Stop
OVER THINKING:

Proven Strategies to Calm Your Mind,
Relieve Stress,
And Overcome Anxiety ~
Break Free and Live in the Moment

Table of Contents

Purpose of the Book

In our fast-paced, information-rich world, overthinking has become an all-too-common habit that can lead to chronic stress and anxiety. As someone who has personally struggled with overthinking, I know the negative effect it can have on mental, emotional, and physical well-being. That's why I wrote "Stop Overthinking: Proven Strategies to Calm Your Mind, Relieve Stress, and Overcome Anxiety - Break Free and Live in the Moment" to shed light on the nature of overthinking, exploring its underlying causes and offer practical strategies to overcome it.

Understanding overthinking is the first crucial step toward addressing it. This book is a supportive hand that delves into the psychological and neurological foundations of overthinking. It's here to help readers recognize its manifestations and triggers in their own lives. By comprehensively examining the detrimental effects overthinking can have—from paralyzing decision-making to straining relationships and compromising health—readers will understand why it is essential to solve this issue head-on.

The primary purpose of this book is to equip readers with practical, actionable strategies to break free from the cycle of overthinking. These strategies are sources of empowerment. For instance, one of the 27 proven techniques is mindfulness meditation, which has been shown to calm the mind and alleviate stress. Another strategy is reframing negative thoughts, a cognitive behavioral technique that can help manage anxiety effectively. Whether through these or other strategies, each empowers readers to live more mindfully and fully in the present moment.

Ultimately, this book aspires to be a comprehensive resource, a trusted companion, for anyone seeking to overcome overthinking and reclaim control over their mental landscape. By understanding the intricacies of overthinking and implementing these practical strategies, readers can pave the way toward a more serene, balanced, and fulfilling life, secure in the knowledge that they have a comprehensive guide.

Author's Journey: Personal Anecdotes and Reasons for Writing the Book

Overthinking has been a relentless companion in my life, a constant presence I've grappled with for as long as I can remember. Nights were spent in a battle with my own thoughts, a marathon of endless possibilities, fears, and what-ifs. Every decision, no matter how trivial, morphed into a Herculean task, laden with self-doubt and second-guessing. This mental whirlpool of overthinking led to a chronic state of stress, seeping into every aspect of my life - my health, relationships, and overall happiness.

There came a moment that served as a wake-up call, a stark realization of the grip overthinking had on my life. I was immobilized by indecision, caught in a web of pros and cons over a seemingly simple choice - whether to accept a new job offer. The list of pros and cons grew longer by the day, and I felt suffocated by my own inability to make a decision. It was no longer just about the job; it was a reflection of how overthinking had taken the reins of my life. At that moment, I knew I had to find a way to break free from this cycle.

My way to conquer overthinking began with hesitant, baby steps. I delved into a myriad of strategies, from mindfulness and meditation to cognitive behavioral techniques. Some methods proved more effective than others, and through a process of trial and error, I started to grasp what truly helped me quieten my mind and regain control. Along the way, I sought the wisdom of professionals, devoured books on the subject, and connected with fellow warriors in this battle against overthinking.

The idea for this book emerged from a deep aspiration to share what I had learned with others who might be struggling with overthinking. I realized that I wasn't alone in this battle and that many people could benefit from the strategies that had helped me transform my life. Writing this book became a mission to provide a comprehensive, practical guide for anyone seeking to overcome overthinking, relieve stress, and find lasting peace.

The strategies I've gathered and the insights I've gained are all here to serve one purpose: to help you break free from overthinking. This book is a testament to my commitment to providing a comprehensive, practical guide for anyone seeking to overcome overthinking, relieve stress, and find lasting peace. It's a beacon of hope and guidance, ready to accompany you on your journey towards mental calm and clarity.

What Readers Will Gain: Overview of Key Takeaways and Benefits

In "Stop Overthinking: Proven Strategies to Calm Your Mind, Relieve Stress, and Overcome Anxiety - Break Free and Live in the Moment" readers will find a comprehensive toolkit designed to address the pervasive issue of overthinking. Here's what you can expect to gain from this book:

1. **Understanding Overthinking**: Gain a deep understanding of what overthinking is, its causes, and how it affects your mental and physical well-being. By recognizing the triggers, you can identify and address them effectively.

2. **27 Proven Strategies**: Discover 27 practical, evidence-based strategies to help calm your mind, relieve stress, and overcome anxiety. These strategies are clearly explained and easy to implement, allowing you to find the best techniques.

3. **Mindfulness and Meditation**: Learn how to include mindfulness and meditation into your daily routine to foster a sense of calm and presence. These practices can help you break free from the cycle of overthinking and live more fully in the moment.

4. **Cognitive Behavioral Techniques**: Explore powerful cognitive behavioral techniques to

challenge and change negative thought patterns. These tools will help you develop healthier thinking habits and resilience against stress and anxiety.

5. **Relaxation Techniques**: Discover various relaxation techniques, like breathing exercises, that can help you quickly reduce stress and achieve a state of relaxation.

6. **Practical Stress Management**: Understand how to manage your time and organize your life to reduce overwhelm and stress. Learn valuable tips for prioritization, scheduling, and creating a more balanced lifestyle.

7. **Healthy Living**: Explore the connection between physical health and mental well-being. Find out how regular exercise, a balanced diet, and proper sleep hygiene can significantly impact your ability to manage stress and anxiety.

8. **Building a Support Network**: Recognize the importance of social support and learn how to develop and maintain a strong support network. Effective communication and setting healthy boundaries will help you cultivate meaningful connections.

9. **Professional Help and Therapies**: Gain insight into when and how to seek professional help. Understand the various therapeutic options available, like cognitive behavioral therapy (CBT) and dialectical behavior therapy (DBT),

and how they can support your journey.

10. **Cultivating Gratitude and Positivity**: Learn daily practices to cultivate gratitude and positivity, which will help you change the focus from negative thoughts to positive experiences.

11. **Embracing Imperfection**: Discover the power of embracing imperfection and letting go of perfectionism. Accepting and learning from mistakes can free you from the constant pressure to be perfect and allow you to live more authentically.

12. **Sustainable Practices**: Create a personalized plan for long-term change. Learn how to maintain progress, handle setbacks, and continue growing towards a more peaceful and present-focused life.

By the end of this book, readers will gain a comprehensive understanding of overthinking and access a diverse set of tools designed to address it. The strategies presented aim to help calm the mind, relieve stress, and manage anxiety more effectively, reducing the impact of overthinking and promoting a more present-focused way of living.

Part 1: Understanding Overthinking

Chapter 1: What is Overthinking?

Definition and Types of Overthinking

Overthinking can be described as continuously analyzing, scrutinizing, and dwelling on thoughts, often to the point where it becomes detrimental to one's mental and emotional well-being. It's the habit of thinking about something too much or for too long, leading to excessive worry, indecision, and feeling overwhelmed. Overthinking is not merely a momentary pause to ponder a difficult decision; it is a persistent and often paralyzing cycle of thoughts that can affect every aspect of life.

There are two primary types of overthinking:

Ruminating: This involves replaying past events repeatedly, focusing on what went wrong, what you wish you had done differently, or feeling regretful about specific actions. Ruminating leads to feelings of sadness, guilt, and depression, as it traps individuals in a loop of negative thinking about past experiences. *For example, Sarah attended a social event where she felt she didn't make a good impression. Days later, she* *still replays the conversations in her mind, thinking about how she could have said something different. This constant rumination leaves her feeling anxious and self-critical.*

Worrying: This type involves overthinking about future events, potential problems, or worst-case scenarios. Worrying is characterized by anxiety and fear about what might happen, leading to constant stress and a feeling of being on edge. It often involves creating multiple hypothetical situations and dwelling on possible adverse outcomes.
John, for instance, has a presentation at work next week. Instead of preparing calmly, he worries incessantly about everything that could go wrong. He imagines the projector failing, his mind going blank, and his colleagues judging him harshly. This persistent worrying keeps him up at night and affects his ability to focus during the day.

Common Signs and Symptoms

Recognizing the signs and symptoms of overthinking is the first step toward addressing it. While everyone experiences occasional bouts of overthinking, chronic overthinkers exhibit certain behaviors and thought patterns that are more intense and frequent. Here are some common signs and symptoms:

1. **Difficulty Making Decisions**: Overthinkers often need help making even simple decisions

because they get caught up in analyzing every possible outcome, leading to indecision and procrastination. *For example, Lisa spends an hour deciding what to wear each morning. She considers how her coworkers might perceive each outfit, whether it's appropriate for the weather, and if she'll still like it by the end of the day.* It leads to unnecessary stress and lateness.

2. **Constant Worrying**: Persistent worry about the future is a hallmark of overthinking. This worry can be about anything from personal relationships to career choices. *Mark constantly worries about his financial situation despite his stable job and savings. He imagines scenarios where he loses his job and can't pay his bills, which causes him ongoing stress despite his security.*

3. **Replaying Past Events**: Overthinkers frequently replay past conversations or events in their minds, analyzing what was said or done and wishing they had acted differently. It often leads to feelings of regret and self-criticism. *After a meeting where Jane presented her ideas, she spent hours thinking about each colleague's reaction, wondering if they liked her proposal, and criticizing herself for not mentioning specific points.*

4. **Inability to Relax**: Overthinkers' constant mental activity makes it difficult to relax and unwind. Their minds always race, making it hard to enjoy downtime or sleep peacefully. *Emma finds it impossible to relax after work.*

Even while watching TV, her mind drifts to the unfinished tasks and upcoming deadlines, preventing her from enjoying the moment.

5. **Physical Symptoms**: Overthinking may lead to physical symptoms such as headaches, fatigue, and digestive issues as the body reacts to the constant stress and anxiety. *Alex often experiences tension headaches and an upset stomach, which his doctor attributes to stress. These physical symptoms are a direct result of his habit of overthinking.*

6. **Avoidance Behavior**: To escape the discomfort of overthinking, individuals may avoid situations or decisions that trigger their anxiety, leading to missed opportunities and restricted life. *Rebecca avoids social gatherings because she fears she won't know what to say and will make a fool of herself. This avoidance prevents her from building relationships and enjoying social interactions.*

7. **Negative Self-Talk**: Overthinkers often engage in negative self-talk, criticizing themselves for perceived mistakes or shortcomings. This internal dialogue can erode self-esteem and contribute to a cycle of negative thinking. *Mike frequently tells himself he's not good enough or intelligent enough whenever he faces a challenge at work, which undermines his confidence and performance.*

Understanding these symptoms is crucial in recognizing overthinking in your life. By becoming aware of how overthinking manifests, you can begin to manage it and find ways to cope with stress and anxiety. This book will provide the tools and strategies to break free from overthinking and live a more balanced and fulfilling life.

Self-Assessment Questions

To help identify whether you are overthinking, consider asking yourself the following questions:

- Do I often find myself replaying past events in my mind?
- Do I struggle to make decisions, even small ones?
- Do I focus on the negative aspects of situations?
- Do I frequently worry about what others think of me?
- Do I experience physical symptoms like headaches or muscle tension related to stress?
- Do I procrastinate because I fear making mistakes or failing?
- Does my constant worrying affect my work, relationships, or daily activities?

Chapter 2: The Science Behind Overthinking

Overthinking is a common phenomenon that affects countless individuals, leading to a cycle of stress and anxiety that can be difficult to break. To effectively address and manage overthinking, it is essential to understand the underlying psychological and neurological mechanisms. This chapter delves into the science behind overthinking, exploring the psychological and neurological explanations as well as the role of stress and anxiety.

Psychological Explanations

Cognitive Theories

Cognitive theories suggest that overthinking, also known as rumination, is rooted in maladaptive thought patterns. These patterns often develop as a response to negative experiences or stress. Cognitive-behavioral therapy (CBT) identifies several cognitive distortions that contribute to overthinking:

- **Catastrophizing**: This involves imagining the worst-case scenario in any given situation, leading to excessive worry and anxiety.
- **Overgeneralization**: Drawing broad, negative conclusions based on a single event, reinforcing a cycle of negative thinking.
- **Mind Reading**: Assuming others think negatively about themselves without concrete

evidence, fostering insecurity and further overthinking.

Understanding these distortions is crucial in identifying and addressing the root causes of overthinking.

Perfectionism and Control

Perfectionism and the need for control are significant psychological factors contributing to overthinking. Individuals with perfectionistic tendencies often set unattainably high standards for themselves, leading to constant self-evaluation and criticism. It can result in an unending loop of overthinking as they strive to meet unrealistic expectations.
Similarly, a strong desire for control can exacerbate overthinking. When individuals feel uncertain or unable to control outcomes, they may excessively think to regain control, even if it is only imaginary.

Neurological Explanations

Brain Structures and Functions

Overthinking involves several brain regions and neural networks. Key areas implicated in this process include:

- **Prefrontal Cortex (PFC)**: The PFC is responsible for higher-order cognitive functions, including decision-making and problem-solving. Overactivity in the PFC can lead to excessive analysis and rumination.
- **Amygdala**: The amygdala processes emotions, particularly fear and anxiety. Heightened

activity in the amygdala can trigger overthinking as a response to perceived threats.
- **Default Mode Network (DMN)**: The DMN is a network of active brain regions during passive, reflective thought. Overactivity in the DMN is associated with increased rumination and self-referential thinking.

Neurotransmitters

Neurotransmitters, the chemical messengers in the brain, also play a crucial role in overthinking. Imbalances in neurotransmitters such as serotonin, dopamine, and norepinephrine can contribute to mood disorders and anxiety, which in turn fuel overthinking.
- **Serotonin**: Low levels of serotonin lead to depression and anxiety, both of which can exacerbate overthinking.
- **Dopamine**: While dopamine is associated with reward and motivation, imbalances can lead to obsessive thinking and compulsive behaviors.
- **Norepinephrine**: This neurotransmitter is involved in the body's stress response. Elevated levels can increase arousal and anxiety, promoting overthinking.

The Role of Stress and Anxiety

Stress Response

Stress activates the body's fight-or-flight response, releasing stress hormones such as cortisol and adrenaline.

While this response is beneficial in acute, life-threatening situations, chronic stress can have harmful effects on mental health. Prolonged exposure to stress hormones can alter brain function, increasing the likelihood of overthinking.

- **HPA Axis**: The hypothalamic-pituitary-adrenal (HPA) axis regulates the stress response. Chronic activation of the HPA axis can lead to heightened anxiety and overthinking.
- **Cortisol**: High levels of cortisol, the primary stress hormone, can impair cognitive function and increase rumination.

Anxiety Disorders

Anxiety disorders like generalized anxiety disorder (GAD) and obsessive-compulsive disorder (OCD) are closely linked to overthinking. These conditions involve persistent, excessive worry that can be difficult to control. Individuals with anxiety disorders often experience disturbing thoughts and compulsive behaviors, which can perpetuate overthinking.

- **GAD**: Characterized by chronic worry about various aspects of life, leading to a continuous cycle of overthinking.
- **OCD**: Involves intrusive, unwanted thoughts (obsessions) and repetitive behaviors (compulsions) aimed at reducing anxiety, often resulting in persistent overthinking.

Breaking the Cycle

Understanding the psychological and neurological foundations of overthinking is the first step toward breaking the cycle. By recognizing cognitive distortions, addressing perfectionistic tendencies, and managing stress and anxiety, individuals can develop effective strategies to calm their minds and live in the moment.

The following chapters will explore practical techniques and strategies to combat overthinking, drawing on scientific research and proven therapeutic approaches. By applying these strategies, you can learn to manage your thoughts, reduce stress, and ultimately break free from the grip of overthinking.

This chapter has provided an overview of the science behind overthinking, highlighting the psychological and neurological mechanisms as well as the role of stress and anxiety. Armed with this knowledge, you are better equipped to understand the root causes of overthinking and take steps toward a calmer, more present state of mind.

Chapter 3: Impact of Overthinking

Effects on Mental and Physical Health

Overthinking can have profound effects on both mental and physical health, often creating a vicious cycle where each aspect exacerbates the other. Here are some real-life examples to illustrate these impacts:

Mental Health:

1. **Anxiety and Depression**: Overthinking leads to anxiety and depression. *For example, Rachel constantly worries about her performance at work. She replays conversations with her boss, fearing she said something wrong. This persistent anxiety makes her feel overwhelmed and unable to enjoy her free time. Eventually, she begins to feel hopeless about ever escaping these thoughts, leading to depression.*

2. **Insomnia**: Overthinking can make it difficult to sleep. *Sam lies awake at night, thinking about everything he needs to do the next day and worrying about potential problems. This lack of sleep affects his mood and cognitive function, making him more prone to further overthinking and stress.*

3. **Cognitive Fatigue**: Constantly thinking about various scenarios and outcomes can lead to cognitive fatigue. *As a university student, Emma*

spends hours daily thinking about her studies, social interactions, and future career. This mental exhaustion makes it harder for her to focus and retain information, impacting her academic performance.

Physical Health:

1. **Headaches and Migraines**: The stress and tension caused by overthinking can lead to frequent headaches and migraines. *Alex, who constantly worries about his family's financial situation, often experiences tension headaches that make it hard for him to concentrate and enjoy daily activities.*

2. **Digestive Issues**: Overthinking can cause digestive problems such as irritable bowel syndrome (IBS). *Lisa experiences stomach cramps and bloating whenever she is stressed about her job. Her overthinking about work-related issues triggers these physical symptoms, creating a cycle of discomfort and worry.*

3. **Weakened Immune System**: Chronic stress from overthinking can break the immune system, making the body more susceptible to illnesses. *For instance, Mark notices that he catches colds more frequently during periods when he's overthinking his career path and future, indicating the toll it's taking on his physical health.*

Consequences on Daily Life and Relationships

Overthinking affects individual health and has significant consequences on daily life and relationships.

Daily Life:

1. **Procrastination**: Overthinkers often procrastinate because they are paralyzed by indecision. *Jane spends so much time weighing the pros and cons of each task that she delays essential work. This procrastination leads to missed deadlines and increased stress.*

2. **Reduced Productivity**: Constantly second-guessing decisions and analyzing every detail can reduce productivity. *Tom, a software developer, finds himself stuck in a loop of refining his code, unable to finalize and submit his work. It reduces his overall productivity and impacts his career progression.*

3. **Lack of Enjoyment**: Overthinking can rob people of the ability to enjoy the present moment. *Sarah goes on a vacation but spends the entire time worrying about what might go wrong back home. As a result, she doesn't fully enjoy her trip and returns feeling just as stressed as before.*

Relationships:

1. **Communication Breakdown**: Overthinking can lead to miscommunication and relationship misunderstandings. *Emma constantly*

overanalyzes her partner's words and actions, often jumping to negative conclusions. It leads to unnecessary arguments and a communication breakdown.

2. **Emotional Distance**: Overthinkers may become emotionally distant as they get lost in their thoughts. *John's constant worry about his job makes him less present in his relationship. His partner feels neglected and unimportant, causing tension and emotional distance between them.*

3. **Dependency on Reassurance**: Overthinkers often seek constant reassurance from loved ones, which can strain relationships. *Lisa frequently asks her friends and family for validation about her decisions, making them feel overwhelmed and frustrated. This dependency can create imbalance and resentment in relationships.*

Understanding the impact of overthinking on mental and physical health and its consequences on daily life and relationships is crucial in recognizing the need to address this issue. By becoming aware of these effects, individuals can take proactive steps to manage their thoughts and improve their overall well-being. This book will provide the tools and strategies needed to break free from the cycle of overthinking, helping readers lead healthier, more fulfilling lives.

Part 2: 27 Proven Strategies to Calm Your Mind

Chapter 4: The 5 AM Club and Meditation: Transforming Your Mornings

Introduction to the 5 AM Club

The concept of the 5 AM Club, popularized by leadership and personal development expert Robin Sharma, revolves around the idea that waking up at 5 AM and following a structured morning routine can improve productivity, mental health, and overall well-being. By dedicating the early hours of the day to self-improvement activities, you can set a positive tone for the rest of your day and, ultimately, your life.

Benefits of the 5 AM Club

1. **Increased Productivity**: Early mornings allow you to focus on essential tasks and set a productive tone for the rest of the day.
2. **Mental Clarity**: Starting your day with activities that promote mental clarity, such as meditation, can help you maintain focus and calm throughout the day.

3. **Physical Health**: Exercise in your morning routine boosts your energy levels, improves physical health, and sets a positive tone for the day.
4. **Emotional Well-Being**: Taking time for personal growth and reflection can enhance your emotional well-being, reduce stress, and increase happiness.

The 20/20/20 Formula with Meditation

Robin Sharma's 20/20/20 formula is a simple yet powerful structure to guide your morning routine. It involves spending the first hour of your day on three key activities, each lasting 20 minutes. Incorporating meditation into this routine can enhance benefits and help you develop a more mindful and present-focused mindset.

1. **Move (5:00 AM - 5:20 AM)**: Exercise to boost energy levels. It could be a quick workout, a run, or even some yoga. Exercise releases endorphins, improving your mood and setting a positive tone for the day.
2. **Meditate (5:20 AM—5:40 AM):** Spend 20 minutes calming your mind and setting a focused, peaceful tone for the day. This could involve mindful breathing, a body scan, or a guided meditation.
3. **Grow (5:40 AM - 6:00 AM)**: Dedicate 20 minutes to personal growth activities such as reading, listening to podcasts, or learning something new. This time is an investment in your personal development and knowledge.

Strategy 1: Mindful Breathing Meditation

Mindful breathing is a simple, powerful technique to calm the mind and reduce overthinking. Here's how to practice conscious breathing:

1. **Find a Comfortable Position**: Sit or lie down in a comfortable position. Close your eyes if you feel comfortable doing so.
2. **Take a Deep Breath**: Inhale deeply, allowing your abdomen to rise. Hold your breath for a moment.
3. **Exhale Slowly**: Exhale slowly, allowing your abdomen to fall. Pay attention to the sensation of your breath as it moves in and out of your body.
4. **Focus on Your Breath**: Continue to breathe deeply and slowly. Focus your attention on your breath. Observe the feeling of the air filling your lungs and leaving your body.
5. **Observe Your Thoughts**: Don't judge yourself for getting distracted; this is a normal part of the process.
6. **Practice Regularly**: Point to practice mindful breathing for a few minutes each day. Gradually increase the duration as you become more comfortable with the practice.

Strategy 2: Body Scan Meditation

Body scan meditation is a method that helps you progress greater awareness of your body and release tension. Here's how to practice a body scan meditation:

1. **Find a Quiet Space**: Lie down on your back comfortably. Close your eyes and take a few deep breaths.
2. **Focus on Your Feet**: Bring your attention to your feet. Notice any sensations you feel, such as warmth, coolness, or tingling. If you don't feel anything, that's okay too. Just observe.
3. **Move Up Your Body**: Gradually move your attention up your body, focusing on each part in turn. Spend a few moments on each area, noticing any sensations or tension. Move from your feet to your legs, hips, abdomen, chest, arms, hands, neck, and head.
4. **Release Tension**: As you focus on each part of your body, imagine breathing into that area and releasing any tension as you exhale. Visualize the stress melting away with each breath.
5. **Stay Present**: If your mind starts to wander, bring your focus back to the part of your body you are currently scanning. Remember, the goal is not to achieve anything specific but to remain present and aware.
6. **Complete the Scan**: After scanning your body, take a few deep breaths and return your attention to the present moment. Open your eyes and take a moment to notice how you feel.

Strategy 3: Guided Meditation

Guided meditation involves listening to a narrator who leads you through the meditation process. It can benefit beginners or those who find it challenging to meditate independently. Here's how to get started with guided meditation:

1. **Choose a Guided Meditation**: Many resources are available, including apps, websites, and audio recordings. Choose a meditation that suits your needs and preferences. Popular apps like Headspace, Calm, and Insight Timer offer a variety of guided meditations.
2. **Find a Quiet Space**: As with other forms of meditation, find a quiet space where you can sit or lie down comfortably.
3. **Follow the Instructions**: Play the guided meditation and follow the narrator's instructions. They will guide you through the process, often including relaxation, breathing, and visualization steps.
4. **Stay Open and Receptive**: Allow yourself to be guided without judgment. If your mind wanders, gently focus on the narrator's voice.
5. **Reflect on Your Experience**: After the meditation, take a few moments to reflect on how you feel. Observe any changes in your mental or emotional state.
6. **Practice Regularly**: Incorporate guided meditation into your routine. Even a few minutes each day can seriously impact your overall well-being.

Enhancing Your Meditation Practice

To deepen your meditation practice and enhance its benefits, consider the following tips:

1. **Create a Relaxing Environment**: Set up a dedicated space for meditation that is quiet and free from distractions. Soft lighting and comfortable seating, such as lavender or chamomile, can enhance the atmosphere.
2. **Use Relaxing Music or Nature Sounds**: Listening to peaceful music or nature sounds can help you relax and focus during meditation. Many meditation apps offer background music or soundscapes to enhance your practice.
3. **Incorporate Aromatherapy**: Essential oils such as lavender, sandalwood, or frankincense can promote relaxation and deepen your meditation experience. Use a diffuser or apply a small amount of diluted essential oil to your pulse points before meditating.
4. **Practice Visualization**: Visualization can be a highly powerful tool for relaxation. Imagine a calm scene, such as a beach or forest, and immerse yourself in the details. It can help you let go of stress and focus your mind.
5. **Combine Meditation with Movement**: Yoga or tai chi integrates mindfulness with physical movement. These activities can help you connect with your body and mind, enhancing the overall benefits of meditation.
6. **Set an Intention**: Before meditation, set a positive intention or focus for your practice. It could be cultivating gratitude, finding inner peace, or letting go of stress. Revisit this

intention throughout your meditation to keep your mind centered.

Integrating the 5 AM Club and meditation into your daily routine allows you to develop a more present-focused mindset, reduce overthinking, and enhance your overall well-being. These strategies offer powerful tools to calm your mind, relieve stress, and manage anxiety, helping you break free from the cycle of overthinking and live more fully in the moment.

Chapter 5: Cognitive Behavioral Techniques

Cognitive Behavioral Therapy (CBT) is a practical approach to managing overthinking. It empowers you to identify and challenge negative thought patterns, replacing them with healthier, more constructive ways of thinking. This chapter delves into three practical CBT strategies: Thought Records, Cognitive Restructuring, and Socratic Questioning. These tools are your key to breaking the cycle of overthinking and cultivating a more balanced and positive mindset, putting you in control of your thoughts and emotions.

Identifying and Challenging Negative Thought Patterns

The first step in combating overthinking is to understand and challenge the negative thought patterns that fuel it. These thoughts, often automatic and deeply ingrained, can significantly impact your mood and behavior. But by recognizing them, you can begin to question their validity and replace them with more rational and positive thoughts. This process brings a sense of relief and opens the door to a more hopeful and optimistic mindset.

Strategy 4: Thought Records

Thought Records are a powerful tool for identifying and examining negative thought patterns. This structured method helps you capture your thoughts, analyze them, and develop more balanced perspectives. Here's how to use Thought Records:

1. **Record the Situation**: Write down the situation that triggered your negative thoughts. Be specific about the context and details.
   - **Example**: "I gave a presentation at work and felt my colleagues were disengaged."

2. **Identify Your Thoughts**: List the automatic thoughts that went through your mind during the situation. These thoughts often reflect your immediate reactions and beliefs.
   - **Example**: "They think I'm boring. I'm not good at presentations. I'm going to lose my job."

3. **Rate Your Emotions**: Note your emotions and rate their intensity on a scale of 0 to 10.
   - **Example**: Anxiety (8), Embarrassment (7), Self-doubt (9).

4. **Examine the Evidence**: Challenge your negative thoughts by examining the evidence for and against them.
   - **Evidence for**: "A few people were looking at their phones."

- **Evidence against**: "Several colleagues nodded and smiled. My manager complimented my presentation afterward."

5. **Develop Alternative Thoughts**: Create more balanced and realistic thoughts based on the evidence.
   - **Example**: "Some people might have been distracted, but others were engaged. My manager's feedback was positive, so I probably did a good job."

6. **Re-rate Your Emotions**: After developing alternative thoughts, re-rate the intensity of your emotions.
   - **Example**: Anxiety (4), Embarrassment (3), Self-doubt (2).

Strategy 5: Practical Exercises for Cognitive Restructuring

Cognitive restructuring involves changing negative thought patterns by challenging them and replacing them with more positive and realistic ones. Here are some practical exercises to help you restructure your thoughts:

1. **Catch It, Check It, Change It**:
   - **Catch It**: Notice when you have a negative thought.
   - **Check It**: Ask yourself if the thought is rational and supported by evidence.

- **Change It**: Replace the negative thought with a more positive and realistic one.

2. **Example**:
   - **Catch It**: "I always mess up at work."
   - **Check It**: "Is it true that I always mess up? What evidence do I have?"
   - **Change It**: "I've had successful projects and positive feedback. I can learn from my mistakes and improve."

3. **Positive Reframing**:
   - Identify a negative thought and find a way to reframe it positively.
   - **Example**: Negative Thought: "I failed at my diet today."
   - **Positive Reframe**: "I had a setback today, but I've been doing well overall. Tomorrow is a new opportunity to make healthier choices."

4. **Perspective Shifting**:
   - Consider how someone else might view the situation.
   - **Example**: Negative Thought: "My friend didn't reply to my message; she must be upset with me."
   - **Perspective Shift**: "My friend might be busy or distracted. It doesn't necessarily mean she's upset with me."

Strategy 6: Socratic Questioning

Socratic Questioning is a method of asking guided questions to challenge and reframe negative thoughts. This technique helps you examine the validity of your thoughts and consider alternative perspectives. Here's how to practice Socratic Questioning:

1. **Clarify the Thought**:
   - **Example**: "I'm not good enough to succeed at this job."
2. **Ask Questions to Challenge the Thought**:
   - **What evidence do I have that supports this thought?**
     - **Example**: "I made a mistake in my last project."
   - **What evidence do I have that contradicts this thought?**
     - **Example**: "I've received positive feedback from my manager and completed several projects successfully."
   - **Is there an alternative explanation?**
     - **Example**: "Making a mistake doesn't mean I'm not good enough; it means I'm human and have room to learn and grow."
   - **What would I tell a friend who had this thought?**
     - **Example**: "I'd remind them of their accomplishments and encourage them to focus on their strengths."
3. **Develop Balanced Thoughts**:

- Based on your answers, create a more balanced and realistic thought.
- **Example**: "I've had both successes and setbacks in my job. I can learn from my mistakes and continue to improve."

4. **Reflect on the Impact**:
    - Notice how the new thought affects your emotions and behavior.

Example of Socratic Questioning:

- **Negative Thought**: "I'll never be able to manage my anxiety."

- **Probing Questions**:
    - What evidence do I have that this thought is true? (I've struggled with anxiety for years.)
    - What evidence do I have that this thought is not true? (I've had periods where I managed my anxiety well.)
    - What are the consequences of holding this thought? (It makes me feel hopeless and prevents me from trying new strategies.)
    - What are the potential benefits of changing this thought? (I could feel more hopeful and motivated to manage my anxiety.)
    - How would I view this situation if I were an objective observer? (I'd see that managing anxiety is a gradual process with ups and downs.)

- **Balanced Thought**: "Managing anxiety is challenging, but I've had success in the past and can continue to find effective strategies."

By incorporating these transformative Cognitive Behavioral Techniques into your daily routine, you can identify and challenge negative thought patterns, reduce overthinking, and develop a more positive and balanced mindset. This journey towards greater mental clarity, emotional well-being, and resilience is possible and within your reach. Let these strategies inspire and motivate you to take control of your thoughts and emotions.

Chapter 6: Relaxation Techniques

Relaxation techniques are essential tools for managing overthinking, stress, and anxiety. They help calm the mind, reduce physical tension, and promote well-being. This chapter will explore three powerful relaxation techniques: Progressive Muscle Relaxation, Guided Imagery, and Relaxation Games. Each technique offers a unique approach to achieving a state of relaxation and can be easily imported into your daily routine.

Strategy 7: Progressive Muscle Relaxation

Progressive Muscle Relaxation (PMR) is a technique that involves tensing and then slowly relaxing different muscle groups in the body. This method helps reduce physical tension and promotes a deep state of relaxation.

Steps for Progressive Muscle Relaxation:

1. **Find a Comfortable Position**: Sit or lie in a comfortable, quiet place where you won't be disturbed.
2. **Focus on Your Breath**: Take a few deep breaths to center yourself and begin the relaxation process.
3. **Tense and Relax Muscle Groups**: Starting from your toes, tense each muscle group for 5-10 seconds, then slowly release the tension and relax for 15-20 seconds before moving to the

next muscle group.

- **Feet and Toes**: Curl your toes tightly, then relax.
- **Calves**: Tighten your calf muscles, then relax.
- **Thighs**: Squeeze your thigh muscles, then relax.
- **Abdomen**: Tense your abdominal muscles, then relax.
- **Chest**: Tighten your chest muscles, then relax.
- **Arms and Hands**: Clench your fists, tighten your arm muscles, and relax.
- **Shoulders**: Shrug your shoulders up towards your ears, then relax.
- **Face**: Scrunch your facial muscles, then relax.

4. **Focus on Relaxation**: After completing all muscle groups, take a few moments to focus on the feeling of relaxation spreading throughout your body. Breathe deeply and enjoy the sensation of complete relaxation.

Strategy 8: Guided Imagery

Guided imagery is a relaxation technique that visualizes calming, peaceful scenes or experiences. Using your imagination, you can create a mental escape from stress and anxiety, promoting a sense of tranquility.

Steps for Guided Imagery:

1. **Find a Quiet Space**: Sit or lie in a comfortable, quiet place where you won't be disturbed. Close your eyes and take a few deep breaths to relax.
2. **Choose a Calming Image**: Think of a place or scene that makes you feel peaceful and relaxed. It could be a beach, a forest, a meadow, or a serene setting.
3. **Visualize the Scene**: Use all your senses to imagine the scene in detail. Picture the colors, shapes, and textures. Listen to the sounds, smell the scents, and feel the sensations.
4. **Engage with the Image**: Imagine yourself fully immersed in the scene. Walk around, touch objects, or sit and enjoy the environment.
5. **Stay in the Moment**: Spend 5-10 minutes in your imagined scene, feeling completely relaxed and at peace.
6. **Return Slowly**: When ready, slowly bring your awareness back to the present moment. Open your eyes and take a few deep breaths, feeling calm.

Example Guided Imagery Script:

The Beach

Imagine yourself on a warm, sandy beach. Feel the sun on your skin and the gentle breeze. Listen to the waves and seagulls screaming above. Smell the salty sea air. Walk along the shoreline, feeling the sand between your toes and the water lapping at your feet. As you sit down, feel the warmth of the sand beneath you and watch the waves gently roll in and out.
Allow yourself to relax completely, feeling calm and at peace.

The Garden

Imagine yourself in a beautiful, private garden with blooming flowers and lush greenery. The air is warm and fragrant with the scent of roses, jasmine, and lavender. You hear the gentle trickle of a fountain and the soft chirping of birds. Walking along the winding paths, you feel a sense of calm and happiness. You find a cozy bench under a flowering arbor and sit down, feeling the sun on your face and the cool shade on your back. You watch butterflies dance from flower to flower and listen to the soothing sounds of nature. Take a few moments to enjoy the peace and beauty of the garden, feeling completely relaxed and at ease.

The Forest
Imagine yourself walking through a deep, green forest.
The air is cool and fresh, filled with pine and earth. You
hear the rustling of leaves in the breeze and the sound
of a babbling brook. Walking along the soft, mossy
path, you notice the sunlight filtering through the
canopy, creating dappled patterns on the ground. Birds
chirp happily in the trees, and you feel a sense of
tranquility and connection to nature. You find a
comfortable sitting spot and leaning against a sturdy
tree, feeling its rough bark against your back. Take a
few moments to breathe deeply and absorb the peaceful
atmosphere of the forest.

The Meadow
Visualize yourself in a vast, open meadow filled with
colorful wildflowers. The sky is light blue, with fluffy
white clouds drifting lazily by. The sun shines warmly
on your face, and a gentle breeze carries the honeyed
fragrance of flowers. Butterflies flutter from blossom to
blossom, and you can hear the soft hum of bees. You
walk through the meadow, feeling the soft grass
beneath your feet. You come across a small, clear pond
and sit by its edge. The water is calm, reflecting the sky
and surrounding flowers. Sitting there, you feel a deep
sense of peace and relaxation, wholly immersed in the
meadow's beauty.

The Mountain

Picture yourself standing at the base of a majestic mountain. The air is crisp and cool, filled with the scent of pine trees. As you begin your ascent, you feel the solid ground beneath your feet and the strength in your legs. You take your time, enjoying the journey and the breathtaking views. The path winds through a forest, and you hear the sounds of birds and leaves. As you climb higher, reveal stunning vistas of valleys and distant peaks. You reach a lookout point and pause to take in the panoramic view. The vastness and beauty of the landscape fill you with a sense of awe and serenity. You find a comfortable spot to sit, feeling the cool breeze and basking in the tranquility of the mountains.

The Ocean

Visualize yourself standing at the edge of a wide, tranquil ocean. The water is a deep blue, and the waves gently lap at the shore. The sky above is clear and endless, and you can feel the sun's warmth on your skin. Walking along the sandy beach, you feel the cool, wet sand between your toes. The sound of the waves is rhythmic and calming, like a natural lullaby. You find a comfortable spot to sit and watch the waves roll in and out. The horizon stretches endlessly before you, and you feel a profound sense of peace and connectedness to the world around you. Let the soothing sights and sounds of the ocean wash over you, bringing a deep understanding of relaxation.

Strategy 9: Games to Reduce Overthinking

While traditional strategies like mindfulness, meditation, and cognitive behavioral techniques effectively manage to overthink, incorporating games can also be a powerful tool. Games can divert attention from negative thought patterns, stimulate the mind positively, and provide a fun and engaging method to cultivate mindfulness and relaxation. This chapter explores various games that can help stop overthinking and promote mental well-being.

Types of Games to Reduce Overthinking

1. **Puzzle Games**

Puzzle games challenge the brain, promoting concentration and problem-solving skills. They require focus and attention, which can help divert the mind from overthinking.

- **Examples**:
    - **Sudoku**: This number puzzle game enhances logical thinking and concentration.
    - **Crossword Puzzles**: These improve vocabulary and problem-solving skills.
    - **Jigsaw Puzzles**: Putting pieces together to form a complete picture requires focus and can be a meditative activity.

2. **Strategy Games**

Strategy games require planning and decision-making, helping to shift focus away from unproductive thoughts to more constructive thinking.

- **Examples**:
    - **Chess**: This classic game enhances strategic thinking and concentration.
    - **Settlers of Catan**: A board game that involves resource management and strategy.
    - **Risk**: This game of global domination requires careful planning and strategy.

3. **Mindfulness and Relaxation Games**

These games are explicitly designed to promote mindfulness and relaxation and help calm and reduce anxiety.

- **Examples**:
    - **Flow Free**: A puzzle game where players connect matching colors with pipes, encouraging a state of flow.
    - **Calm (App)**: Includes various relaxing games and activities promoting mindfulness.
    - **Monument Valley**: A visually stunning game that involves navigating through beautiful, illusionary architecture.

4. **Creative Games**

Engaging in creative activities should reduce stress and promote a sense of accomplishment and joy, which can counteract overthinking.

- **Examples**:
    - **Minecraft**: Allows players to build and explore the virtual world, fostering creativity and focus.
    - **Coloring Books (Apps or Physical)**: Digital and physical coloring books can be calming and therapeutic.
    - **The Sims**: A life simulation game where players can create and manage virtual characters and environments.

5. **Physical Activity Games**

Games that involve physical activity can help release endorphins, reduce stress, and promote overall well-being.

- **Examples**:
    - **Dance Revolution**: A game that combines music and movement to get players dancing and moving.
    - **Wii Sports**: Includes various sports simulations that encourage physical activity.

Here are some tips:

1. **Set Aside Time for Play**: Dedicate specific times during the day for playing games. It can be a great way to unwind after work or as a break during stressful periods.

2. **Choose Games You Enjoy**: Select games that you find enjoyable and engaging. The goal is to divert your mind from overthinking, so choose games that captivate your interest.
3. **Play with Friends or Family**: Social interaction can enhance the positive effects of gaming. Playing games with friends or family will support and create positive experiences.
4. **Combine with Other Techniques**: Use games with other mindfulness and cognitive behavioral techniques. For example, you can play a relaxing game after a mindfulness meditation session.
5. **Monitor Your Screen Time**: While games can be beneficial, balancing screen time with other activities is essential. Ensure you maintain a healthy balance of physical activity, social interaction, and relaxation.

Examples of Using Games to Combat Overthinking

- **Sudoku**:

If you are overthinking at the end of the day, start solving Sudoku puzzles for 15 minutes before bed. It helps focus on something enjoyable and challenging, easing her mind and improving sleep quality.

- **Chess**:

    You mindfully engage in the game when you strategize and plan your moves. It reduces the tendency to ruminate about work stress and other worries.

- **Coloring**:

The coloring helps to relax and disconnect from anxious thoughts, making you feel refreshed and focused for the rest of the day.

- **Dance Games**:
Physical activity combined with fun and upbeat music lifts the mood and reduces anxiety, helping you feel more energized and positive.

Using these relaxation methods in your daily routine can help you manage overthinking, reduce stress, and promote a sense of calm. Progressive muscle relaxation, guided imagery, and relaxation games are helpful tools that can be used individually or in combination to achieve a state of relaxation and well-being.

Chapter 7: Lifestyle Changes

Adopting healthy lifestyle habits can significantly reduce overthinking and promote overall well-being. This chapter explores three key strategies: regular exercise, a balanced diet, and sleep hygiene. These changes can help you manage stress, improve mental clarity, and enhance emotional resilience.

Strategy 10: Regular Exercise

The Role of Exercise in Stress Management

Regular physical activity is one of the most effective ways to combat stress and overthinking. Exercise boosts the production of endorphins, the body's natural mood elevators. It also helps reduce levels of the stress hormone cortisol, promoting a sense of calm and relaxation.

Benefits of Exercise:

- **Reduces Anxiety and Depression**: Exercise releases neurotransmitters like serotonin and dopamine, which improve mood and relieve symptoms of anxiety and depression.
- **Improves Cognitive Function**: Physical activity enhances brain function, improving memory, attention, and decision-making.

- **Promotes Better Sleep**: Regular exercise helps regulate sleep patterns, leading to more restful and restorative sleep.
- **Increases Energy Levels**: Exercise boosts energy and reduces feelings of fatigue, making it easier to tackle daily tasks.

Practical Tips for Incorporating Exercise:

1. **Find an Activity You Enjoy**: Choose an exercise that you find enjoyable and engaging, whether walking, running, swimming, dancing, or playing a sport.
2. **Set Realistic Goals**: Start with small, achievable goals and gradually increase the intensity and duration of your workouts.
3. **Create a Routine**: Schedule regular exercise sessions at a time that works best for you. Consistency is critical to reaping the benefits of physical activity.
4. **Mix It Up**: Incorporate exercises to keep your routine exciting and target different muscle groups.
5. **Stay Active Throughout the Day**: Look for opportunities to move more, such as taking the stairs, walking during lunch breaks, or doing short home workouts.

Strategy 11: Balanced Diet

The Importance of Nutrition for Mental Health

A balanced diet provides the essential nutrients your brain and body need to function optimally. Poor nutrition can exacerbate stress, anxiety, and overthinking, while a healthy diet can enhance mental clarity, mood, and energy levels.

Critical Nutrients for Mental Health:

- **Omega-3 Fatty Acids**: Fatty fish, flaxseeds, and walnuts contain omega-3s, which support brain health and reduce inflammation.
- **B Vitamins**: Important for energy production and brain function. Sources include whole grains, eggs, leafy greens, and legumes.
- **Magnesium**: Helps regulate stress hormones and promotes relaxation. It is found in nuts, seeds, dark chocolate, and leafy greens.
- **Antioxidants**: Protect the brain from oxidative stress. Rich sources include berries, nuts, and vegetables.

Practical Tips for a Balanced Diet:

1. **Eat a Variety of Foods**: Include a wide range of fruits, vegetables, whole grains, lean proteins, and healthy fats in your diet.
2. **Stay Hydrated**: Drink plenty of water throughout the day to stay hydrated and support overall health.

3. **Limit Processed Foods**: Reduce the intake of processed and sugary foods, negatively impacting mood and energy levels.
4. **Eat Regular Meals**: Maintain a regular eating schedule to keep your energy levels stable and avoid overeating.
5. **Mindful Eating** involves Paying attention to what and how you eat, avoiding distractions during meals, and savoring each bite.

Healthy Recipes:

1. **Omega-3 Power Salad**:

   - **Ingredients**:
     - 2 cups mixed greens (spinach, arugula, kale)
     - 1 avocado, sliced
     - 1 cup cherry tomatoes, halved
     - 1/2 cup walnuts
     - 1/2 cup cooked quinoa
     - 1/2 cup blueberries
     - 1 can (4-6 oz) wild-caught salmon, drained
     - Olive oil and balsamic vinegar for dressing

   - **Instructions**:

a.   In a large bowl, combine the mixed greens, avocado, cherry tomatoes, walnuts, quinoa, and blueberries.

b.   Top with the salmon.

c.   Drizzle with olive oil and balsamic vinegar and toss gently to combine.

d.   Serve immediately.

2. **Magnesium-Rich Smoothie**:

- **Ingredients**:
  - 1 banana
  - 1 cup spinach
  - 1/2 cup Greek yogurt
  - 1 tablespoon almond butter
  - 1 tablespoon chia seeds
  - 1 cup almond milk
  - 1 teaspoon honey (optional)

- **Instructions**:

a.   Combine all ingredients in a blender.
b.   Blend until smooth.
c.   Pour into a glass and enjoy immediately.

Avoid Caffeine and Sugar: Limit Intake to Reduce Anxiety

Many of us, in our fast-paced world, turn to caffeine and sugar to keep up with our busy schedules. While substances can provide a temporary boost in energy, they can also contribute to increased anxiety and overthinking. But here's the empowering part: understanding the impact of caffeine and sugar on your body and mind and learning how to limit your intake can be crucial steps toward reducing anxiety and fostering a calmer, more focused life. You have the power to make these changes and take control of your mental well-being.

The Effects of Caffeine on Anxiety

Caffeine is a stimulant in coffee, tea, energy drinks, and some medications. It blocks adenosine receptors in the brain that help to keep you awake and alert. However, this exact mechanism can also lead to increased heart rate, jitteriness, and anxiety, particularly in individuals who are sensitive to caffeine.

1. Heightened Stress Response: Caffeine can trigger the release of adrenaline, the hormone responsible for the "fight or flight" response. It can lead to feelings of anxiety, especially if consumed in large amounts.

2. Sleep Disruption: Consuming caffeine, especially later in the day, can interfere with sleep patterns. Poor sleep quality is an essential contributor to anxiety and overthinking, creating a vicious cycle, were lack of sleep leads to increased caffeine consumption, further exacerbating anxiety.

3. Increased Heart Rate: The stimulating effects of caffeine can cause an increase in heart rate and palpitations, which can mimic anxiety symptoms and make you feel more anxious.

Reducing Caffeine Intake

When decreasing your caffeine intake, it's best to take it slow. Cutting back too quickly can cause withdrawal symptoms such as headaches, irritability, and fatigue. Instead, try a gradual reduction. For instance, if you usually have three cups of coffee daily, reduce it to two cups, then to one, and eventually switch to decaffeinated options.

Timing Matters: Avoid consuming caffeine in the late afternoon and evening to prevent it from interfering with your sleep. Aim to have your last caffeinated drink by early afternoon.

Explore Alternatives: Try herbal teas, such as chamomile or peppermint, which have calming effects and can help reduce anxiety. Additionally, drink more or infused water with natural flavors like lemon or cucumber to stay hydrated without relying on caffeine.

The Impact of Sugar on Anxiety

Sugar is another common stimulant in many foods and drinks, including sweets, pastries, soft drinks, and even some savory items. While it can provide a quick catch of energy, it also has several adverse effects on mental health.

1. Blood Sugar Spikes and Crashes: Consuming sugar rapidly increases blood sugar levels. These fluctuations can cause feelings of irritability, mood swings, and anxiety.

2. Inflammation: High sugar intake increases inflammation in the body, which can affect the brain and contribute to symptoms of anxiety and depression.

3. Addiction and Cravings: Sugar can be addictive, leading to cravings and overconsumption. The cycle of craving and consumption can contribute to anxiety as you become increasingly dependent on sugar for energy and mood regulation.

Limiting Sugar Intake

1. Read Labels: Read labels carefully to be mindful of hidden sugars in processed foods. Check for high fructose corn syrup, sucrose, dextrose, and all added sugar.

2. Natural Sweeteners: Replace sugar with natural sweeteners like honey or stevia. These alternatives can perform your sweet tooth without causing the same dramatic blood sugar spikes.

3. When you manage your sugar intake, it's not just about avoiding sweets. A balanced diet is key. Focus on fruits, vegetables, proteins and whole gains. These foods provide energy and help regulate blood sugar levels, reducing anxiety and overthinking. By adopting a holistic approach to your diet, you can significantly impact your overall mental health and well-being.

4. Mindful Eating: Practice mindful eating by focusing on your hunger and fullness cues. Avoid eating sugary foods out of boredom or stress, and instead, opt for healthier snacks like nuts, seeds, or yogurt.

By understanding the effects of caffeine and sugar on your body and mind and taking steps to limit your intake, you can reduce anxiety and promote a more balanced, calm lifestyle. Making choices about what you consume can significantly impact your overall mental health and well-being, helping you live in the moment and break free from the cycle of overthinking.

Alcohol and Overthinking: Understanding the Connection

Alcohol is often used as a social lubricant and a way to unwind after a long day. However, while it may seem to reduce stress and anxiety in the short term, alcohol can have significant adverse effects on mental health, particularly about overthinking. Understanding how alcohol influences the brain and body can help you make more informed decisions about its consumption and manage your anxiety more effectively.

How Alcohol Affects the Brain

1. Neurotransmitter Imbalance: Alcohol affects the balance of neurotransmitters in the brain. Initially, it increases the activity of gamma-aminobutyric acid (GABA), a neurotransmitter that produces calming effects and decreases the activity of glutamate, which excites the brain. This imbalance can lead to a temporary feeling of relaxation and euphoria. However, as the effects wear off, the brain tries to restore balance, often resulting in increased anxiety and irritability.

2. Impact on Serotonin: Alcohol can also influence serotonin level, a neurotransmitter that regulates mood. While moderate consumption might initially increase serotonin levels, excessive drinking can lead to a significant drop, contributing to feelings of depression and anxiety.

3. Cognitive Impairment: Alcohol impairs cognitive functions such as memory, decision-making, and concentration. It can exacerbate overthinking as the brain struggles to process information efficiently and make sound decisions.

The Cycle of Overthinking and Alcohol

1. Temporary Relief: Many people turn to alcohol to cope with stress and overthinking. The initial calming effects can provide temporary relief from racing thoughts and anxiety.

2. Rebound Anxiety: Once the effects of alcohol wear off, anxiety and overthinking often return with greater intensity. It is due to the rebound effect, where the brain compensates for the effects of alcohol by increasing excitatory neurotransmitter activity.

3. Increased Overthinking: Alcoholic cognitive impairments can make it harder to process thoughts and emotions rationally, leading to increased overthinking as the brain tries to make sense of the impaired mental state.

4. Dependence and Tolerance: Regular use of alcohol to manage overthinking can lead to tolerance, where more alcohol is needed to achieve the same effects.

Managing Alcohol Consumption to Reduce Overthinking

1. Set Clear Limits: Establish limits on how much and how often you drink. Sticking to these limits can help prevent the damaging effects of alcohol on your mental health.

2. Alcohol-Free Days: Designate certain days of the week as alcohol-free to give your brain and body a chance to recover. It can help break the loop of dependence and reduce overall anxiety levels.

3. Find Alternative Coping Mechanisms: Explore other ways to manage stress and overthinking, such as exercise, meditation, or hobbies. These activities can provide healthier ways to cope with anxiety.

4. Seek Support: If you find it challenging to reduce your alcohol consumption on your own, seek support from friends, family, or a mental health professional. Support groups can provide valuable strategies for managing both alcohol use and anxiety.

5. Stay Hydrated and Nourished: Drinking water and maintaining a balanced diet can help reduce some of the negative effects of alcohol. Dehydration and poor nutrition can exacerbate anxiety and overthinking, so it's essential to take care of your physical health as well.

By understanding the relationship between alcohol and overthinking, you can make more informed decisions about your drinking habits. Limiting alcohol intake and exploring alternative coping mechanisms can significantly reduce anxiety and promote a healthier, more balanced mental state.

Strategy 12: Sleep Hygiene for Mental Clarity

The Importance of Quality Sleep

Quality sleep is essential for mental clarity, emotional stability, and well-being. Poor sleep can lead to increased stress, anxiety, and difficulty concentrating, exacerbating overthinking.

Tips for Improving Sleep Hygiene:

1. **Create a Relaxing Bedtime Routine**: Establish a calming pre-sleep routine to signal your body that it's time to wind down. It could include reading, taking a warm bath, or practicing relaxation exercises.
2. **Maintain a Consistent Sleep Schedule**: Go to bed and wake up simultaneously every day, even on weekends. Consistency helps regulate your body's internal clock.
3. **Create a Sleep-Conducive Environment**: Ensure your bedroom is calm, dark, and quiet. Use blackout curtains, earplugs, or a white noise machine if necessary.
4. **Limit Screen Time Before Bed**: Avoid electronic devices at least an hour before bedtime. The blue light emitted by screens can interfere with your body's production of melatonin, a hormone that regulates sleep.
5. **Watch Your Diet**: Avoid large meals, caffeine, and alcohol before bed, as they can disrupt sleep.

Relaxation Techniques for Better Sleep:

Progressive Muscle Relaxation (PMR)

Purpose: To reduce physical tension and promote relaxation by progressively tensing and relaxing each muscle group.

How to Do It:

1. **Get Comfortable**: Lie down in a comfortable position with your eyes closed.
2. **Start with Your Feet**: Tense the muscles in your feet by curling your toes and holding the tension for 5-10 seconds. Then, relax the muscles and feel the stress melt away.
3. **Move Up Your Body**: Slowly work your way up, tensing and relaxing each muscle group. Move from your feet to your calves, thighs, buttocks, abdomen, chest, arms, hands, neck, and face.
4. **Breathe Deeply**: Take deep, slow breaths as you tense and relax each muscle group. Inhale deeply when tensing and exhale fully when relaxing.

Example:

- **Feet**: Curl your toes tightly and hold for 5-10 seconds. Release and relax.
- **Calves**: Tighten your calf muscles, hold, then relax.
- **Thighs**: Squeeze your thigh muscles, hold, then relax.

Yoga for Sleep

Purpose: To promote relaxation and prepare the body for sleep through gentle yoga poses.

How to Do It:

1. **Child's Pose (Balasana)**:
   - Kneel on the floor, sit back on your heels, and stretch your arms forward, resting your forehead on the ground. Hold for 1-3 minutes.
2. **Legs-Up-the-Wall Pose (Viparita Karani)**:
   - Sit with one side of your body against a wall. Lie back and swing your legs up against the wall. Relax your arms by your sides. Hold for 5-10 minutes.
3. **Corpse Pose (Savasana)**:
   - Lie flat on your back with your arms by your sides and palms facing up. Close your eyes and focus on deep, slow breaths. Hold for 5-10 minutes.

Integrating Lifestyle Changes

Incorporating these lifestyle changes into your daily routine can significantly reduce overthinking and enhance your overall well-being. Here's a sample plan to help you get started:

1. **Morning**:
   - **Exercise**: Start your day with a 30-minute workout, such as jogging, yoga, or a home exercise routine.

- **Breakfast**: Enjoy a balanced breakfast with protein, healthy fats, and whole grains.

2. **Daytime**:
   - **Stay Active**: Take short breaks throughout the day to stretch or walk. Stay hydrated by drinking water regularly.
   - **Healthy Meals**: Eat balanced meals that include a variety of nutrients to maintain energy and focus.

3. **Evening**:
   - **Relaxation**: Wind down with a calming activity, such as reading, meditation, or a warm bath.
   - **Sleep Hygiene**: Follow your bedtime routine and aim for consistent sleep and wake times.

Adopting regular exercise, a balanced diet and good sleep hygiene can create a foundation for reducing overthinking and promoting mental clarity and emotional stability.

Chapter 8: Time Management and Daily Routine Organization

Effective time management and daily routine organization are critical for reducing overthinking and enhancing productivity. Having a clear plan and a well-organized environment makes it easier to focus on tasks, make decisions, and maintain a calm mindset. This chapter explores three key strategies: prioritization techniques, creating a schedule, and decluttering your space.

Strategy 13: Prioritization Techniques to Reduce Overwhelm

Prioritizing tasks is like putting on glasses that help you see clearly what needs to be done. It's like having a map that guides you through a maze of tasks. By focusing on what's most important, you can ensure critical tasks are completed first and you make steady progress toward your goals.

Techniques for Prioritization:

The Eisenhower Matrix:

Description: This technique categorizes tasks into four quadrants based on urgency and importance.

Quadrant 1: Urgent and Important (tasks to do immediately)

Quadrant 2: Not Urgent but Important (tasks to schedule)

Quadrant 3: Urgent but Not Important (tasks to delegate)

Quadrant 4: Not Urgent and Not Important (tasks to eliminate)

Use the Eisenhower Matrix to categorize your tasks for the week. Identify an upcoming project deadline as urgent and vital (Quadrant 1) and a long-term goal of learning a new skill as not urgent but important (Quadrant 2).

The Ivy Lee Method: Write down the six most important tasks to accomplish the next day at the end of each day. Prioritize these tasks and focus on completing one at a time. This method encourages concentrated effort on high-priority tasks and reduces decision fatigue.

Eat That Frog: This technique is like a superhero that swoops in to save your day. It suggests tackling your most challenging task (the 'frog') first thing in the morning. By getting the most difficult task out of the way, you reduce procrastination and its anxiety, freeing up mental space for other activities.

Strategy 14: Creating a Schedule

Creating a structured schedule can help you manage your time more effectively, reduce stress, and ensure you allocate time for essential tasks and self-care.

1. The Bullet Journal: A bullet journal is a simple and effective tool that combines to-do lists, calendars, and journaling into one organized system. This flexible method allows you to customize your planning process, track your progress, and reflect on your goals, helping to reduce overthinking about what needs to be done. With this tool, you can take charge of your time and tasks with ease.

2. Timeboxing: Allocate specific periods to different daily tasks or activities. Setting start and end times for tasks creates a sense of urgency and a clear structure for your day, preventing tasks from dragging on and reducing the tendency to overthink.

3. MITs (Most Important Tasks): Identify your three most important daily tasks. Focus on these tasks first before moving on to less critical activities. This technique ensures that your highest priorities are addressed, reducing the stress of unfinished vital tasks.

Strategy 15: Decluttering Your Space

1. The 30-Day Minimalism Game: Challenge yourself to eliminate one item on the first day, two on the second day, and so on for 30 days. This gradual approach makes decluttering manageable and can significantly reduce the physical and mental clutter contributing to overthinking.

2. The Four-Box Method: When decluttering, use four boxes labeled Keep, Donate, Trash, and Relocate. This technique provides a clear framework for decision-making and helps you systematically tackle cluttered areas without feeling overwhelmed.

3. The One-In, One-Out Rule: For every new item that you bring into your space, remove an old one. This rule helps maintain a balanced environment and prevents the accumulation of unnecessary items, promoting a more precise and focused mind.

Implementing these strategies can enhance your time management and organization skills, ultimately reducing the mental clutter that leads to overthinking. Prioritizing tasks, creating effective schedules, and maintaining a decluttered space are potent steps toward a more tranquil and productive life.

Chapter 9: Social Support and Connection

Social connections are necessary for mental health and happiness. A robust support network can make a valuable difference when facing challenges like overthinking. This chapter explores three key strategies to enhance social support and connection: building a support network, effective communication, and setting boundaries.

Strategy 16: Building a Support Network

A support network is a group of people you can rely on for emotional, practical, and sometimes financial support. Building and maintaining this network is essential for managing stress and reducing overthinking.

Steps to Build a Support Network

1. **Identify Your Needs**: Understand what kind of support you need. Is it emotional support during tough times, practical help with tasks, or advice and guidance?
2. **Reach Out to Friends and Family**: Start with the people you know. Let them know you value their support and are willing to reciprocate.
3. **Join Groups and Communities**: Participate in clubs, organizations, or online communities that

interest you. Shared activities create natural opportunities for connection.
4. **Seek Professional Help**: Sometimes, professional support is necessary. Therapists and support groups can provide valuable assistance.
5. **Be Open and Vulnerable**: Building deep connections requires openness. Share your feelings and experiences honestly and encourage others to do the same.

Tips for Maintaining a Support Network

- **Regular Check-ins**: Keep in touch, even by sending a quick message or calling.
- **Show Appreciation**: Express gratitude for the support you receive.
- **Be a Good Listener**: Support is reciprocal. Be there for others as they are for you.

Strategy 17: Effective Communication

Effective communication is the foundation of solid connections. It helps to prevent misunderstandings, resolve conflicts, and build deeper connections.

Effective Communication to Stop Overthinking

Overthinking often stems from misunderstandings, unresolved conflicts, and internalizing negative thoughts. Effective communication can help mitigate these triggers by fostering clarity, reducing uncertainty, and promoting emotional balance. Here are detailed strategies to use effective communication as a tool to stop overthinking:

Active Listening

Active listening involves fully concentrating on what the other person is saying, understanding their message, responding thoughtfully, and remembering the conversation.

Steps to Practice Active Listening:

1. **Pay Attention**: Give the speaker your undivided attention. Put away distractions like phones and laptops. Make eye contact to show you are engaged.
2. **Show You're Listening**: Use non-verbal cues such as nodding, smiling, and leaning forward. Verbal affirmations like "I see," "I understand," and "Go on" encourage the speaker.
3. **Provide Feedback**: Paraphrase what the speaker has said to confirm understanding. For example, "What I hear you saying is…" or "It sounds like you're feeling…"
4. **Defer Judgment**: Avoid interrupting with counterpoints or judgments. Let the speaker finish their ideas before responding.
5. **Respond Appropriately**: Be honest and respectful in your responses. Acknowledge their

feelings and offer support or solutions if
appropriate.

Clear and Concise Expression

Expressing your thoughts clearly and concisely reduces
misunderstandings that can lead to overthinking.

Techniques for Clear Communication:

1. **Be Direct**: State your message directly and
   avoid beating around the bush. For example,
   instead of saying, "I'm kind of upset about
   earlier," say, "I felt hurt when you interrupted
   me during the meeting."
2. **Use "I" Statements**: Frame your messages
   using "I" statements to show your feelings and
   needs without blaming others. For example, "I
   feel overwhelmed when I'm given last-minute
   tasks" instead of "You always give me tasks at
   the last minute."
3. **Be Specific**: Provide specific details about your
   thoughts and feelings. Instead of saying, "You
   never help out," say, "I noticed you didn't help
   with the dishes last night, and it made me feel
   unsupported."
4. **Stay On Topic**: Try to keep the conversation
   focused on the issue at hand. Avoid bringing up
   unrelated past events or grievances.

Non-Verbal Communication

Non-verbal cues can crucially impact how your
messages are received and understood.

Improving Non-Verbal Communication:

1. **Body Language**: Use open body language to convey openness and receptivity. Avoid crossing your arms or looking away when speaking.
2. **Facial Expressions**: Match your facial expression with your verbal message. Smiling when discussing a serious issue can create confusion.
3. **The tone of Voice**: Your tone can convey emotions and intentions. Aim for a calm and even tone, especially when discussing sensitive topics.
4. **Physical Distance**: Respect personal space to avoid making others feel uncomfortable. Be mindful of cultural contrast in personal space preferences.

Empathy and Understanding

Empathy helps build solid connections and reduces misunderstandings that can lead to overthinking.

Practicing Empathy:

1. **Put Yourself in Their Shoes**: Try to understand the other person's behavior and feelings. Ask yourself how you would feel in their situation.
2. **Validate Their Feelings**: Acknowledge and validate the other person's emotions. For example, "I can see why you would feel that way" or "That sounds challenging."
3. **Ask Questions**: Encourage the others to share their feelings and experiences. Open-ended

questions like "Can you tell me more about
that?" or "How did that make you feel?" show
that you care.

Assertiveness

Being assertive helps you express your needs and
boundaries clearly, reducing the stress and anxiety that
fuel overthinking.

Steps to Being Assertive:

1. **Know Your Rights**: Recognize that your
   feelings and needs are valid and that you have
   the right to express them.
2. **Use "I" Statements**: As mentioned earlier, use
   "I" statements to assert your needs and feelings
   without blaming others.
3. **Practice Saying No**: Understand that it's okay
   to say no. For example, "I'm sorry, but I can't
   take on another project right now."
4. **Stay Calm**: Maintain a calm and respectful
   demeanor, even when asserting yourself. Avoid
   aggressive or passive-aggressive behavior.

Conflict Resolution

Resolving conflicts effectively prevents lingering issues
that can lead to overthinking.

Techniques for Conflict Resolution:

1. **Address Issues Promptly**: Don't let conflicts
   fester. Address them immediately to prevent

them from growing into more significant problems.

2. **Stay Focused on the Issue**: Keep the discussion centered on the issue. Avoid bringing up past grievances or unrelated topics.
3. **Seek Solutions**: Focus on finding mutually agreeable solutions rather than winning the argument. Collaborate to reach a resolution that satisfies both parties.
4. **Agree to Disagree**: Sometimes, it's okay to agree to disagree. Accept that you may not always see eye to eye, and that's perfectly fine.

Reflective Listening

Reflective listening ensures that both parties understand each other, reducing misunderstandings and overthinking.

Practicing Reflective Listening:

1. **Paraphrase**: Restate what the other person has said in your own words. For example, "So what you're saying is…" or "It sounds like you're feeling…"
2. **Clarify**: Ask questions to clarify any points you don't understand. For example, "Can you explain what you mean by…?"
3. **Summarize**: After the conversation, summarize the main points to ensure mutual understanding. For example, "To summarize, we agreed that…"

By incorporating these strategies, you can increase your communication skills, reduce misunderstandings, and prevent the overthinking that often results from poor communication.

Strategy 18: Setting Boundaries

Setting healthy boundaries is critical for maintaining our mental health and preventing overthinking. Boundaries help define what you are comfortable with and how you expect others to treat you.

Steps to Set Healthy Boundaries

1. **Identify Your Limits**: Reflect on your physical, emotional, and mental limits. What are you comfortable with, and what feels too much?
2. **Communicate Clearly**: Clearly express your boundaries to others. Use direct language and be specific about your needs.
3. **Be Consistent**: Stick to your boundaries consistently. Discrepancy can lead to confusion and frustration for both you and others.

4. **Learn to Say No**: Understand that it's okay to say no. Saying no is an essential part of respecting your limits.
5. **Seek Support**: If setting boundaries is challenging, seek support from friends, family, or a therapist.

Tips for Maintaining Boundaries

- **Practice Self-Care**: Regularly engage in activities that replenish your energy and maintain your well-being.
- **Be Respectful**: Respect others' boundaries as you expect them to respect yours.
- **Adjust as Needed**: Boundaries can change over time. Re-evaluate and adjust them as your circumstances and needs evolve.
- **Handle Pushback Calmly**: People may resist your boundaries. Address pushback calmly and reaffirm your limits without feeling guilty.

Boundary Mapping Exercise

The boundary mapping exercise is a powerful tool to help you visually understand and reinforce your boundaries. Other exercises include creating a visual representation of your boundaries and identifying areas where they are challenged. Here's a detailed step-by-step guide on how to perform this exercise:

Materials Needed
- A large piece of paper or a whiteboard
- Markers or pens
- Sticky notes (optional)

Step-by-Step Instructions

1. **Create the Boundary Circle**

   - **Draw a Circle**: Draw a circle in the center of your paper or whiteboard. This circle represents your personal space and boundaries.

- **Label the Circle**: At the top of the circle, write "My Boundaries" to remind yourself of the purpose of this exercise.

2. **Identify Your Boundaries**

- **Physical Boundaries**: Inside the circle, write down your physical boundaries. These include personal space preferences, physical contact limits, and privacy needs.
- **Emotional Boundaries**: Next, list your emotional boundaries. These could encompass limits on what you are willing to share emotionally, how you expect to be treated, and what you are comfortable discussing.
- **Mental Boundaries**: Include your mental boundaries. These involve protecting your mental health and avoiding specific topics that cause distress or limit intellectual debates.
- **Time Boundaries**: Write down your time boundaries, such as your availability, time you need for yourself, and commitments you're willing to make.

3. **Identify Boundary Violators**

- **List Challengers**: Outside the circle, list people, situations, or activities that frequently challenge or violate your boundaries. Use sticky notes if you

prefer a more flexible approach, moving them around as needed.
- **Be Specific**: Be as specific as possible. Instead of writing "work," write down "colleague asking for help after hours" or "boss expecting immediate replies to emails."

4. Analyze Challenges

- **Patterns and Triggers**: Look for patterns in the challenges. Are there specific people or situations that repeatedly cross your boundaries? Identify common triggers that make it challenging to maintain your boundaries.
- **Emotional Responses**: Reflect on how these violations make you feel. Do you experience stress, anxiety, anger, or guilt? Understanding your emotional responses can help you develop strategies to protect your boundaries.

5. Plan Boundary Reinforcement

- **Set Clear Boundaries**: For each item outside the circle, think of clear, assertive boundaries you can set. Write these boundaries inside the circle next to the relevant category (physical, emotional, mental, or time).
- **Communicate Boundaries**: Plan how to communicate these boundaries to the relevant people or in specific situations.

Use "I" statements to assert your needs without placing blame.

> - Example: "I need some quiet time after work to relax, so I won't be able to help with extra tasks after hours."

6. **Practice and Adjust**

   - **Role-Play**: Practice setting and communicating these boundaries with a trusted friend or in front of a mirror. It can help build your confidence.
   - **Review and Adjust**: Revisit your boundary map regularly and adjust it based on new situations.

Reflection and Maintenance

- **Journaling**: Keep a journal to check your progress. Write" down instances where you successfully upheld your boundaries and situations where you struggled. Reflect on what is working well and what can be improved.
- **Seek Support**: Share your boundary map with a trusted friend, family member, or therapist. They can provide feedback and support as you work on reinforcing your boundaries.
- **Self-Care**: Remember that setting boundaries is a form of self-care. Take time to recharge and engage in activities that nurture your well-being.

This exercise helps you clarify your need to feel safe and respected by visually mapping your boundaries and identifying challenges. It also provides a practical framework for asserting and maintaining these boundaries in your daily life.

Chapter 10: Professional Techniques and Therapies

Professional techniques and therapies can effectively manage overthinking, especially when self-help strategies are insufficient. This chapter explores three professional approaches: Exposure Therapy, Dialectical Behavior Therapy (DBT), and the importance of seeking professional help. These therapies can provide structured support and specialized techniques, empowering you to take control and overcome overthinking and related anxiety.

Strategy 19: Exposure Therapy

What is Exposure Therapy?

Exposure Therapy is a psychological technique that helps reduce fears and anxieties. It involves gradually exposing a person to the feared context without any danger to help them overcome their anxiety. This technique is particularly effective for anxiety disorders and phobias.

How Exposure Therapy Works:

1. **Identify Triggers**: The first step in Exposure Therapy is to identify the specific situations, objects, or thoughts that trigger anxiety and overthinking.

- **Example**: Sarah has a fear of public speaking. Her therapist helps her identify that her anxiety peaks when she has to speak in front of a large audience.

2. **Develop a Hierarchy**: Create a list of anxiety-provoking situations, ranked from least to most anxiety-inducing.
   - **Example**: Sarah's hierarchy might start with practicing a speech alone in front of a mirror, followed by a small group of friends, and finally, a large audience.

3. **Gradual Exposure**: Start with the most minor anxiety-provoking situation and gradually work your way up the hierarchy.
   - **Example**: Sarah begins by practicing her speech alone at home. Once she feels comfortable, she moves on to practicing in front of a mirror, and so on.

4. **Use Coping Techniques**: Throughout the exposure process, manage anxiety using coping techniques such as deep breathing, mindfulness, and positive self-talk.
   - **Example**: Sarah practices deep breathing and positive affirmations before and during her exposure exercises.

5. **Review and Reflect**: After each exposure session, review what went well and what can be improved. Reflect on how the anxiety level changed.

- **Example**: After each practice session, Sarah discusses with her therapist what worked and what didn't, adjusting her approach as needed.

Benefits of Exposure Therapy:

1. **Reduces Avoidance Behaviors**: By facing fears directly, individuals learn that their anxiety decreases over time, reducing the tendency to avoid anxiety-provoking situations. This leads to a sense of relief, greater confidence, and freedom in daily life.

2. **Increases Confidence in Handling Anxiety-Provoking Situations**: Gradual exposure helps build resilience and self-efficacy, empowering individuals to handle situations that previously caused distress.

3. **Decreases Overall Anxiety Levels**: Repeated exposure to anxiety triggers without negative consequences helps rewire the brain, reducing the overall intensity of anxiety responses.

4. **Enhances Quality of Life**: As anxiety diminishes, individuals can engage more fully in activities and relationships, improving their overall quality of life.

Strategy 20: Dialectical Behavior Therapy (DBT)

What is Dialectical Behavior Therapy?

Dialectical Behavior Therapy (DBT) is a form of cognitive-behavioral therapy directed to help individuals regulate their emotions, improve interpersonal relationships, develop coping skills, and reduce self-destructive behaviors. DBT is effective for individuals with borderline personality disorder, but it can benefit those struggling with overthinking and anxiety.

Core Components of DBT:

1. **Mindfulness**: Developing awareness of the present moment and accepting it without judgment.
2. **Distress Tolerance**: Learning to tolerate and survive crises without making things worse.
3. **Emotion Regulation**: Understanding and managing intense emotions.
4. **Interpersonal Effectiveness**: Enhancing communication and relationships with others.

DBT Techniques and Practices:

1. **Mindfulness Exercises**: Practice mindfulness meditation daily to increase awareness and acceptance. Spend 10 minutes each morning focusing on your breath and observing your thoughts.

2. **Emotion Regulation Skills**: Identify triggers and use emotion regulation techniques to manage your responses.
3. **Distress Tolerance Tools**: Develop a toolkit of distress tolerance skills for high-stress situations. Create a list of activities that distract you from negative emotions, such as reading a book or walking.
4. **Interpersonal Effectiveness Strategies**: Practice communication skills to improve your interactions with others. Use the DEAR MAN technique (Describe, Express, Assert, Reinforce, Mindful, Appear confident, Negotiate) to handle conflicts assertively.

Benefits of DBT:

1. **Enhances Emotional Regulation**: DBT teaches skills to understand and manage intense emotions effectively, reducing the frequency and intensity of emotional outbursts.
2. **Improves Interpersonal Relationships**: By learning effective communication and relationship skills, individuals can build stronger, healthier relationships with others.
3. **Increases Resilience to Stress**: DBT equips individuals with tools to handle stress and crises without resorting to harmful behaviors, enhancing overall resilience.
4. **Promotes Mindfulness and Acceptance**: Regular mindfulness helps individuals stay present, reducing rumination and overthinking.

Strategy 21: Seeking Professional Help

When overthinking and anxiety become overwhelming, remember that looking for professional help is not a sign of weakness, but a courageous step towards managing your mental health. Mental health professionals can provide evidence-based treatments and personalized care to help you manage the symptoms and improve your quality of life.

Types of Professional Help:

1. **Therapists and Counselors**: Licensed professionals who provide talk therapy to explore your thoughts and feelings. Cognitive-behavioral therapy (CBT) and dialectical behavior therapy (DBT) are common approaches used by therapists to treat overthinking and anxiety.
2. **Psychiatrists**: Doctors specializing in mental health can prescribe medication if needed. A psychiatrist may prescribe anti-anxiety medication or antidepressants to help manage severe symptoms.
3. **Support Groups**: Groups led by trained facilitators where individuals with similar experiences can share and support each other. Joining an anxiety support group can help to reduce feelings of isolation.

Steps to Seek Professional Help:

1. **Recognize the Need**: Acknowledge that overthinking and anxiety affect your daily life and well-being.

2. **Research Options**: Look for qualified mental health professionals in your area or online.
3. **Schedule an Appointment**: Contact a mental health professional to schedule an initial consultation.
4. **Prepare for Your Appointment**: Write down your symptoms, concerns, and questions.
5. **Commit to the Process**: Attend your sessions regularly and be open to the therapeutic process.

Benefits of Seeking Professional Help:

1. **Provides Personalized Care and Support**: Professional therapists offer individualized treatment plans meeting your needs and challenges.
2. **Offers Evidence-Based Treatments**: Therapists and psychiatrists use scientifically validated methods to treat anxiety and overthinking, increasing the likelihood of successful outcomes.
3. **Helps Develop Coping Strategies and Skills**: Professional help provides practical tools and techniques to manage anxiety and reduce overthinking.
4. **Reduces Symptoms of Anxiety and Overthinking**: Effective therapy can decrease the intensity and frequency of anxiety and overthinking, improving overall quality of life.
5. **Enhances Self-Awareness and Insight**: Therapy encourages self-reflection and helps to gain a deeper understanding of emotions and thoughts.

Part 3: Overcoming Anxiety

Chapter 11: Understanding Anxiety

Anxiety is a common and natural human experience, but it can become overwhelming and debilitating if not properly managed. Understanding anxiety and how it differs from everyday stress is the first step in overcoming it. This chapter explores the distinctions between anxiety and stress, common triggers, and the various manifestations of anxiety. Furthermore, we will connect these concepts to overthinking, explaining how they interact and exacerbate each other.

Differentiating Between Anxiety and Everyday Stress

What is Stress?

Stress is the body's natural response to a perceived threat or challenge. It is typically short-term but can be beneficial in certain situations by helping you stay alert and focused. Stress triggers the "fight-or-flight" response, releasing hormones like adrenaline and cortisol that balance your body to respond to immediate danger.

Characteristics of Stress:

- **Short-term**: Stress usually resolves once the situation causing it is over.
- **Specific Trigger**: Stress is often linked to a particular situation, such as a work deadline, an argument, or a financial problem.
- **Physical Symptoms**: Common symptoms include increased heart rate, sweating, muscle tension, and rapid breathing.
- **Motivational**: In moderate amounts, stress can motivate you to take action and solve problems.

What is Anxiety?

Anxiety, on the other hand, is a persistent feeling of worry or fear that can be disproportionate to the actual threat. Unlike stress, anxiety can linger even after the stressor is gone and can occur without any obvious trigger. It often involves excessive worry about future events and can interfere with daily functioning.

Characteristics of Anxiety:

- **Long-term**: Anxiety can persist for weeks, months, or even years.
- **Generalized**: Anxiety might not be linked to a specific event and can be pervasive across various aspects of life.
- **Emotional Symptoms**: Symptoms include excessive worry, restlessness, irritability, and difficulty concentrating.
- **Debilitating**: Anxiety can be overwhelming and hinder daily activities, relationships, and overall quality of life.

Critical Differences Between Stress and Anxiety:

- **Duration**: Stress is typically short-term, while anxiety is long-term.
- **Triggers**: Stress has identifiable triggers, whereas anxiety might not.
- **Impact**: Stress can motivate and be resolved through action; anxiety often feels paralyzing and harder to alleviate.

Common Triggers of Anxiety:

1. **Work-Related Stress**:
   - **Examples**: High workloads, tight deadlines, job insecurity, and conflicts with colleagues or supervisors.
   - **Manifestations**: Excessive worry about job performance, fear of failure, and dread of going to work.
2. **Health Concerns**:
   - **Examples**: Chronic illness, fear of disease, or significant health changes.
   - **Manifestations**: Hypochondria, excessive checking of symptoms, and constant worry about health.
3. **Financial Issues**:
   - **Examples**: Debt, job loss, unexpected expenses, and economic instability.
   - **Manifestations**: Persistent worry about money, fear of not meeting financial obligations and avoidance of financial planning.

4. **Personal Relationships**:
    - **Examples**: Conflicts with family or friends, relationship breakups, and social pressures.
    - **Manifestations**: Fear of rejection, excessive need for reassurance, and avoidance of social situations.
5. **Major Life Changes**:
    - **Examples**: Moving, starting a new job, getting married, or having a baby.
    - **Manifestations**: Overwhelming worry about the future, fear of the unknown, and difficulty adjusting to change.
6. **Traumatic Events**:
    - **Examples**: Abuse, accidents, natural disasters, and witnessing violence.
    - **Manifestations**: Flashbacks, hypervigilance, and avoidance of reminders of the trauma.

Manifestations of Anxiety:

1. **Physical Symptoms**:
    - **Heart Palpitations**: Feeling your heart race or pound in your chest.
    - **Sweating**: Excessive sweating, especially in stressful situations.
    - **Muscle Tension**: Chronic tension in the neck, shoulders, or back.
    - **Fatigue**: Feeling constantly tired despite adequate rest.
    - **Digestive Issues**: Stomachaches, nausea, and irritable bowel syndrome.
2. **Cognitive Symptoms**:

- **Excessive Worry**: Persistent and uncontrollable worry about various aspects of life.
  - **Racing Thoughts**: Inability to control or slow down rapid and overwhelming thoughts.
  - **Difficulty Concentrating**: Trouble focusing on tasks or following conversations.
  - **Catastrophizing**: Always expecting the worst possible outcome.
3. **Emotional Symptoms**:
  - **Restlessness**: Unable to relax.
  - **Irritability**: Becoming easily frustrated or annoyed.
  - **Fear and Panic**: Intense and sudden feelings of terror or impending doom.
  - **Depression**: Feeling sad, hopeless, or worthless.
4. **Behavioral Symptoms**:
  - **Avoidance**: Avoiding situations or places that can trigger anxiety.
  - **Procrastination**: Delaying tasks due to fear of failure or overwhelming worry.
  - **Compulsive Behaviors**: Engaging in repetitive actions to alleviate anxiety, such as checking or counting.
  - **Isolation**: Withdrawing from social interactions and activities.

Example Scenario: Mark is a software engineer who recently started experiencing anxiety symptoms. At work, he feels overwhelmed by tight deadlines and complex projects. At home, he constantly worries about his performance and fears losing his job. Mark notices

physical symptoms like heart palpitations and muscle
tension and cognitive symptoms like racing thoughts
and difficulty concentrating. These symptoms affect his
sleep and overall well-being, prompting him to seek
help.

Simple Decision Steps:

1. **Recognize the Problem**: Mark realizes that his
   anxiety is affecting his work and home life.

2. **Seek Professional Help**: He decides to consult
   a therapist who can help him manage his
   anxiety.

3. **Therapeutic Techniques**:

   - **Cognitive-Behavioral Therapy (CBT)**:
     Mark learns to identify and change
     negative thoughts.

   - **Relaxation Techniques**: He practices
     deep breathing and muscle relaxation
     exercises.

   - **Mindfulness**: Mark incorporates
     mindfulness meditation into his routine
     to stay calm.

4. **Improve Sleep Hygiene**: He establishes a
   regular sleep schedule and creates a calming
   bedtime routine.

5. **Time Management**: Mark uses techniques like
   prioritization and time blocking to manage his
   workload effectively.

6. **Social Support**: He talks to friends and family for support and considers joining a support group.

Connecting Anxiety to Overthinking

The Vicious Cycle of Anxiety and Overthinking

Anxiety and overthinking are closely related and often exacerbate each other. Overthinking can be a symptom of anxiety, while stress can trigger patterns of overthinking, creating a vicious cycle that is difficult to break.

1. **How Overthinking Fuels Anxiety**:
    - **Constant Worry**: Overthinking involves dwelling on potential problems and worst-case scenarios, which fuels anxiety.
    - **Indecisiveness**: Excessive analysis can make decisions difficult, increasing uncertainty and anxiety.
    - **Rumination**: Overthinking past events or mistakes can cause persistent worry and regret, heightening anxiety levels.

2. **How Anxiety Fuels Overthinking**:
    - **Hypervigilance**: Anxiety can make you overly alert and sensitive to potential threats, leading to constant over-analysis.
    - **Catastrophizing**: Anxiety often involves expecting the worst outcomes,

which can drive obsessive thinking about potential failures or dangers.

- **Avoidance**: Anxiety can cause avoidance of certain situations, leading to more time spent ruminating and overthinking.

Breaking the Cycle:

1. **Awareness**: Recognizing when you are caught in the cycle of anxiety and overthinking is the first step. Pay attention to your thoughts and emotions.
2. **Mindfulness**: Practice mindfulness to stay grounded in the moment. Mindful breathing or body scans can help interrupt the cycle.
3. **Cognitive Restructuring**: Challenge irrational thoughts and replace them with more balanced perspectives. Cognitive Behavioral Therapy (CBT) techniques can be particularly effective.
4. **Set Limits on Worry**: Allocate a specific "worry time" each day to address concerns and use the rest of your time for productive activities and relaxation.
5. **Physical Activity**: Regularly exercise to reduce stress and improve mental clarity.

By understanding the differences between anxiety and everyday stress, identifying common triggers, recognizing the various manifestations of anxiety, and learning how they connect to overthinking, you can begin to address and manage these challenges more effectively.

Chapter 12: Anxiety-Specific Strategies

Anxiety, often intertwined with overthinking, can be a debilitating condition. However, by addressing anxiety directly, you can significantly alleviate overthinking and improve your overall mental health. This chapter will empower you with three anxiety-specific strategies: Gradual Exposure Techniques, Desensitization Practices, and Relaxation Response. Each plan offers a unique approach to managing anxiety and can be tailored to your individual needs, giving you the control and capability to manage your condition.

Strategy 22: Gradual Exposure Techniques

Gradual exposure techniques involve systematically and progressively exposing oneself to anxiety-provoking stimuli. The goal is to reduce fear behaviors by facing and becoming desensitized to the sources of anxiety.

Steps for Gradual Exposure Techniques:

1. **Identify Triggers**: List specific situations, objects, or thoughts that provoke anxiety. Rank them in order of least to most anxiety-inducing.
2. **Create an Exposure Hierarchy**: Arrange the triggers in a hierarchy, starting with the least

anxiety-provoking and gradually progressing to the most challenging.

3. **Start with the Least Anxiety-Provoking**: Begin exposure with the least anxiety-inducing item on your list. Spend time in the presence of this trigger until your anxiety begins to decrease.

4. **Gradually Increase Exposure**: Move up the hierarchy, gradually exposing yourself to more challenging triggers. Take your time and ensure that your anxiety decreases with each step before moving on.

5. **Use Relaxation Techniques**: To help manage anxiety, employ relaxation strategies, like deep breathing or muscle relaxation, during and after exposure.

Example:

- **Trigger**: Public speaking.
- **Exposure Hierarchy**:
    - Practice speaking in front of a mirror.
    - Record yourself speaking and watch the playback.
    - Practice speaking in front of a close friend or family member.
    - Give a short presentation to a small, supportive group.
    - Deliver a speech to a larger audience.

Strategy 23: Desensitization Practices

Desensitization practices aim to reduce anxiety responses by repeatedly exposing individuals to anxiety-provoking stimuli in a controlled and systematic manner. It can be particularly effective for phobias and specific anxieties.

Steps for Desensitization Practices:

1. **Relaxation Training**: Before desensitization, learn and practice relaxation techniques to manage anxiety during exposure.
2. **Create a Fear Hierarchy**: Like gradual exposure, list and rank anxiety-provoking stimuli from least to most frightening.
3. **Start with Visualization**: Begin desensitization by imagining the least anxiety-provoking situation while practicing relaxation techniques.
4. **Gradually Progress to Real-Life Exposure**: Once you can visualize the situation without significant anxiety, progress to real-life exposure. Start with the least anxiety-provoking and progressively move to more challenging conditions.
5. **Repeat and Reinforce**: Repeat exposure sessions regularly until the anxiety response diminishes. Reinforce progress by rewarding yourself for successful exposures.

Example:
- **Fear**: Fear of flying.
- **Fear Hierarchy**:
    - Visualize booking a flight.

- Watch different videos of airplanes taking off and landing.
- Visit an airport to observe planes.
- Take a short, local flight with a supportive friend or family member.
- Gradually progress to longer flights.

Strategy 24: Relaxation Response

The relaxation response is a condition of deep rest that counteracts the body's stress response. Practicing techniques to elicit a relaxation response can reduce anxiety.

Steps for Eliciting the Relaxation Response:

1. **Choose a Relaxation Technique**: Select a method that works best for you, such as deep breathing, progressive muscle relaxation, or guided imagery.
2. **Find a Quiet Space**: Choose a quiet, comfortable place where you won't be disturbed.
3. **Focus on Your Breath**: Close your eyes and take slow, deep breaths. Focus on breath entering and leaving your body.
4. **Repeat a Word or Phrase**: With each exhale, repeat a word or phrase calming to you, such as "relax" or "peace."
5. **Visualize a Calming Scene**: Imagine a peaceful scene, such as a beach or forest, and fully immerse yourself in the visualization.

6. **Practice Regularly**: Aim to practice the relaxation response for 10-20 minutes daily to build resilience against anxiety.

By incorporating these anxiety-specific strategies, you can effectively manage and reduce anxiety, ultimately alleviating overthinking. Gradual exposure techniques, desensitization practices, and the relaxation response are potent tools that can lead you to a calmer, more balanced state of mind when used individually or in combination.

Part 4: Breaking Free and Living in the Moment

Chapter 13: Cultivating Gratitude and Positivity

Cultivating gratitude and positivity is a transformative passage, a path that leads to liberation from overthinking and a gateway to a more mindful life. This chapter delves into three potent strategies to ignite this transformation: Daily Gratitude Practices, Positive Affirmations, and Journaling for Reflection. By weaving these techniques, you can shift your focus from negative to positive thoughts, enhancing your overall well-being.

Strategy 25: Daily Gratitude Practices

Gratitude, a practice of acknowledging and appreciating the good in your life, is a powerful tool that can shift your attention away from what you lack to what you have. This shift in focus promotes a positive outlook, leading to a more fulfilling and mindful life. Here's how you can incorporate daily gratitude practices into your life:

1. **Morning Gratitude Ritual**: Start your day with three things you are grateful for. This will set a positive tone and help you focus on the good.

2. **Gratitude Journal**: Start a journal where you write down things you are grateful for daily. It can be as simple as good weather or as profound as a meaningful conversation.
3. **Gratitude Jar**: Place a jar prominently in your home. Write something you are pleasant for each day on a slip of paper and put it in the jar. Over time, the jar will fill with positive reminders of your blessings.
4. **Express Gratitude to Others**: Take the time to thank the people in your life. Whether it's a heartfelt note or a simple "thank you," expressing gratitude can strengthen your relationships and boost your mood.

Practicing gratitude daily can transform your perspective, making it easier to navigate challenges and appreciate the present moment.

Strategy 26: Positive Affirmations

Positive affirmations, powerful statements that challenge negative thoughts and promote self-belief, have the potential to transform your mindset. Regularly repeating positive affirmations can rewire your brain to focus on positive thoughts. Here's how to effectively use positive affirmations:

1. **Identify Negative Thoughts**: Recognize the negative thoughts that frequently occupy your mind. These could be self-doubts, fears, or worries.

2. **Create Positive Affirmations**: Transform these negative thoughts into positive affirmations. For example, if you often think, "I can't handle this," reframe it to, "I am capable and strong enough to handle this."
3. **Daily Practice**: Repeat your positive affirmations daily. Say them out loud, write them down, or even set reminders on your phone.
4. **Believe in Your Affirmations**: It is essential to believe in the affirmations you repeat. Visualize them accurately and feel the emotions associated with them.
5. **Use Visual Cues**: Place your affirmations where you can see them often, such as on your bathroom mirror, desk, or phone's lock screen.

When you redirect your attention from negative to positive thoughts through affirmations, you are taking a powerful step towards building self-confidence and fostering a more optimistic outlook. This practice empowers you to shape your own mindset, putting you in control of your thoughts and emotions.

Examples of Positive Affirmations

Positive affirmations are powerful tools for cultivating a positive mindset and overcoming negative thoughts. Here are some examples you can incorporate into your daily routine:

General Positive Affirmations

1. I am worthy of love and respect.
2. I believe in myself and my abilities.

3. I am in control of my thoughts and emotions.
4. I am capable of achieving my goals.
5. I am grateful for the abundance in my life.
6. I am growing and learning every day.
7. I deserve happiness and success.
8. I am surrounded by positivity and peace.
9. I trust the process of life.
10. I am a strong, independent person.

Health and Wellness Affirmations

1. I am healthy, strong, and vibrant.
2. I nourish my body with healthy choices.
3. I prioritize my mental and physical well-being.
4. I am full of energy and vitality.
5. I listen to my body and respect its needs.
6. I am grateful for my healthy body and mind.
7. I am in harmony with the natural rhythm of life.
8. I choose to be kind to myself.
9. I am calm, relaxed, and peaceful.
10. I am constantly improving my health and wellness.

Career and Success Affirmations

1. I am confident in my skills and abilities.
2. I attract success and abundance.
3. I am open to new opportunities and experiences.
4. I am dedicated and passionate about my work.
5. I am successful in whatever I do.
6. I am a valuable asset to my team.
7. I am focused and persistent in achieving my goals.
8. I am constantly learning and growing professionally.

9. I embrace challenges as opportunities for growth.
10. I am making a positive impact in my career.

Relationships and Social Affirmations

1. Loving and supportive people surround me.
2. I communicate openly and honestly with others.
3. I attract positive and healthy relationships.
4. I am a good friend and a great listener.
5. I deserve to be treated with love and respect.
6. I give and receive love effortlessly.
7. I am patient, kind, and understanding.
8. I create meaningful connections with those around me.
9. I respect the boundaries of others and my own.
10. I am grateful for the love and support I receive.

Personal Growth and Self-Love Affirmations

1. I am constantly evolving and becoming my best self.
2. I embrace my authenticity and celebrate my individuality.
3. I am proud of who I am and who I am becoming.
4. I forgive myself for past mistakes and learn from them.
5. I am deserving of all the good things life has to offer.
6. I trust myself to make the right decisions.
7. I am confident and comfortable in my skin.
8. I am worthy of achieving my goals.
9. I am at peace with who I am.

10. I love and accept myself unconditionally.

Incorporate these positive affirmations by repeating them in the morning, writing them down, or placing them where you can see them often. Over time, these affirmations can help reframe your mindset, reduce overthinking, and promote a more positive and fulfilling life.

Strategy 27: Journaling for Reflection

Journaling is a tool for self-reflection and self-discovery. It provides a space to process your thoughts, understand your emotions, and gain profound insights into your behavior. Here's how to embark on this tour of self-discovery through journaling for reflection:

1. **Set Aside Time**: Highlight a time each day for journaling. It could be in the morning to set purposes or in the evening to reflect on your day.
2. **Free Writing**: Allow yourself to write without worrying about grammar or structure. Let your thoughts flow onto the paper, capturing whatever comes to mind.
3. **Prompt-Based Journaling**: Use prompts to guide your journaling. Prompts like "What am I proud of today?" or "What challenges did I face and how did I overcome them?" can help focus your reflection.
4. **Reflect on Your Entries**: Regularly review your journal entries to check patterns in your

thoughts and behaviors. It will help you understand your triggers and develop strategies to manage them.

5. **Set Goals and Intentions**: Use your journal to set goals and intentions for personal growth. Focus on your progress and adjust your strategies as needed.

Journaling for reflection can help you gain clarity, process your emotions, and foster a deeper understanding of yourself. It can ultimately aid in your trip to break free from overthinking and live in the moment.

Cultivating gratitude and positivity through daily practices, positive affirmations, and reflective journaling can significantly impact your mental well-being. Integrating these strategies into your life allows you to shift your focus from negative to positive thoughts, enhance your self-awareness, and build a more fulfilling, mindful existence.

Chapter 14: Embracing Imperfection

In a world that often glorifies perfection, the pressure to be flawless can be overwhelming and lead to chronic overthinking. Embracing imperfection is liberating and essential for personal growth and happiness. This chapter dives into the importance of accepting and learning from mistakes and letting go of perfectionism.

Accepting and Learning from Mistakes

The Value of Mistakes

Mistakes are a natural part of life and an invaluable source of learning. They offer opportunities for growth, self-improvement, and resilience. By accepting mistakes, you can shift your perspective from viewing them as failures to seeing them as steppingstones towards success.

Steps to Accept and Learn from Mistakes:

1. **Acknowledge the Mistake**:
   - **Description**: Recognize that you have made a mistake without self-judgment.
   - **Example**: Instead of criticizing yourself for missing a deadline, acknowledge that it happened and accept it as a part of your learning process.
2. **Analyze the Cause**:

- **Description**: Reflect on what led to the mistake and identify contributing factors.
- **Example**: Reflect on whether poor time management, lack of resources, or miscommunication contributed to missing the deadline.

3. **Extract Lessons**:
   - **Description**: Determine what you can learn from the mistake to avoid repeating it in the future.
   - **Example**: Learn that setting realistic deadlines and improving communication with your team can help prevent similar issues.

4. **Develop a Plan for Improvement**:
   - **Description**: Create a concrete plan to implement the lessons learned and improve your approach.
   - **Example**: Plan to use a project management tool to stay on deadlines and schedule regular check-ins with your team.

5. **Forgive Yourself**:
   - **Description**: Let go of self-blame and be compassionate with yourself.
   - **Example**: Remember that everyone makes mistakes and that self-compassion is crucial for personal growth.

6. **Move Forward**:
   - **Description**: Apply what you've learned and focus on future opportunities rather than dwelling on the past.

- **Example**: Use the lessons learned to meet future deadlines and improve your overall productivity successfully.

Benefits of Accepting Mistakes:

- **Reduced Anxiety**: Accepting mistakes minimizes the fear of failure, alleviating anxiety.
- **Enhanced Resilience**: Learning from mistakes builds resilience and adaptability.
- **Increased Confidence**: Overcoming and learning from mistakes boosts self-confidence and self-efficacy.

Letting Go of Perfectionism

The Perils of Perfectionism

Perfectionism involves setting unrealistically high standards and being overly critical of oneself. While doing level best is commendable, perfectionism can lead to chronic stress, procrastination, and a persistent fear of failure.

Steps to Let Go of Perfectionism:

1. **Set Realistic Goals**:
   - **Description**: Establish attainable and realistic goals that challenge you without being unattainable.
   - **Example**: Instead of aiming for a perfect presentation, strive to deliver a clear and

engaging talk.

2. **Prioritize Progress Over Perfection**:
    - **Description**: Focus on making progress and improving incrementally rather than achieving perfection.
    - **Example**: Celebrate the completion of each draft of your project and seek feedback for improvement rather than striving for a perfect final version immediately.

3. **Embrace Imperfection**:
    - **Description**: Accept that imperfection is a natural part of life and that flaws can be valuable.
    - **Example**: Acknowledge that a few mistakes in your work do not diminish its overall quality or your abilities.

4. **Practice Self-Compassion**:
    - **Description**: Treat yourself with kindness and understanding, especially when you make mistakes.
    - **Example**: Instead of harshly criticizing yourself for a mistake, offer encouragement and remind yourself of your strengths.

5. **Limit Comparison**:
    - **Description**: Avoid comparing yourself to others and focus on your growth and achievements.
    - **Example**: Recognize that everyone has their own pace and way, and focus on

your progress rather than measuring yourself against others.

6. **Adopt a Growth Mindset**:
   - **Description**: Embrace a mindset that values learning and growth over achieving fixed outcomes.
   - **Example**: View challenges and setbacks as opportunities to learn and grow rather than threats to your self-worth.

Additional Techniques to Support Letting Go of Perfectionism

Letting go of perfectionism can be challenging but rewarding. Here are several more techniques to help you cultivate a more balanced approach to life.

1. **Self-reflection and Journaling**

Purpose: Encourages introspection and awareness of perfectionist tendencies, helping to identify and address them.
Practice:
   - **Daily Reflection**: Set aside time daily to reflect on your experiences, thoughts, and feelings. Write about moments when you felt the urge to be perfect and analyze what triggered these feelings.
   - **Prompt Questions**: Use prompt questions like "What did I do well today?" "What can I learn from today's challenges?" and "How can I be kinder to myself?" to guide your journaling.

2. Set SMART Goals

Purpose: Helps create clear, attainable goals that are specific, measurable, achievable, relevant, and time-bound, reducing the pressure of perfectionism.
Practice:
- **Specific**: Clarify what you want to achieve.
    - **Example**: Instead of "I want to be better at work," set a goal like "I want to improve my project management skills."
- **Measurable**: Ensure the goal can be tracked and measured.
    - **Example**: "I will complete a project management course by the end of the month."
- **Achievable**: Set realistic and attainable goals.
    - **Example**: "I will dedicate 30 minutes daily to study for the course."
- **Relevant**: Align the goal with your broader objectives.
    - **Example**: "Improving my project management skills will help me advance in my career."
- **Time-bound**: Set a deadline for the goal's achievement.
    - **Example**: "I will complete the course by the 30th of this month."

3. Embrace Imperfection in Creative Activities

Purpose: Engaging in creative activities allows you to experiment, make mistakes, and see the beauty in imperfection.
Practice:

- **Creative Projects**: Take up a hobby like painting, writing, or crafting where the focus is on expression rather than perfection.
  - **Example**: Join a painting class where the goal is to enjoy the process rather than create a perfect masterpiece.
- **Celebrate Mistakes**: View mistakes as a natural part of the creative process and an opportunity for growth.
  - **Example**: If you make an error in your painting, incorporate it into the artwork rather than starting over.

4. Practice Vulnerability

Purpose: Embracing vulnerability helps you accept your imperfections and build authentic connections with others.

Practice:

- **Share Your Struggles**: Tell trusted friends or family about your perfectionist tendencies and challenges.
  - **Example**: Share with a friend how your perfectionism affects your work-life balance.
- **Accept Feedback**: Be open to constructive criticism and use it as a tool for growth rather than a measure of your worth.
  - **Example**: Ask for feedback on a project and focus on how you can improve rather than taking it as a personal failure.

5. Limit Social Media Consumption

Purpose: Reducing exposure to curated and often unrealistic portrayals of perfection on social media can decrease feelings of inadequacy and perfectionism.
Practice:

- **Set Boundaries**: Control the time you spend on social media platforms.
    - **Example**: Allocate specific times during the day for social media use and stick to them.
- **Curate Your Feed**: Follow accounts that promote authenticity and self-acceptance rather than perfection.
    - **Example**: Unfollow accounts that make you feel inadequate and follow those that inspire self-love and personal growth.

6. **Graded Exposure to Imperfection**

Purpose: Gradually expose yourself to situations where you allow imperfection, helping to reduce anxiety and increase comfort with being less than perfect.
Practice:

- **Start Small**: Begin with low-stakes situations and gradually move to more significant ones.
    - **Example**: Leave a typo in an email and observe the outcome. Gradually progress to more critical tasks where you allow for minor imperfections.
- **Reflect on Outcomes**: After each exposure, reflect on the results and reinforce the understanding that imperfection is acceptable.
    - **Example**: Notice that leaving a typo didn't have severe consequences and use this realization to build confidence in allowing imperfection in more

significant tasks.

Embracing imperfection is a decisive step toward reducing overthinking and improving mental well-being. By accepting and learning from mistakes and letting go of perfectionism, you can cultivate resilience, boost self-confidence, and lead a more balanced and fulfilling life.

Chapter 15: Building a Sustainable Practice

Creating a Personalized Plan for Long-Term Change

Overcoming overthinking is not a quick fix but a way of long-term change. It's about developing new habits and strategies you can sustain over time. Overthinking can be a chronic habit that affects your mental and physical well-being. Creating a personalized plan customized to your needs and lifestyle is essential to break free from this cycle. Here are the steps to develop a sustainable plan for long-term change:

Self-Assessment
Start by conducting a self-assessment to identify the triggers and patterns of your overthinking. A self-assessment is a process of reflecting on your thoughts, feelings, and behaviors to gain insights into what causes your overthinking. Keep a journal to record instances when you are overthinking, noting the time, place, and situation. Track your thoughts and feelings to understand what causes your overthinking.

Set Clear Goals

Define what you want to achieve by overcoming overthinking. Goals should be specific, achievable, and time bound. For example, instead of saying, "I want to stop overthinking," set a goal like "I want to reduce overthinking by practicing mindfulness for 10 minutes daily over the next three months."

Choose Appropriate Strategies

Select strategies that resonate with you and fit your lifestyle. Some effective techniques include:

- **Mindfulness and Meditation**: Regular practice, such as taking a few deep breaths and focusing on the present moment, can help you stay present and reduce rumination. For instance, when you find yourself overthinking about a past event, you can bring your attention back to the present by focusing on your breath or the sensations in your body.
- **Cognitive Behavioral Techniques**: Challenge and reframe negative thoughts.
- **Relaxation Techniques**: Engage in progressive muscle relaxation or guided imagery to calm your mind.
- **Time Management and Organization**: Prioritize tasks and create a structured schedule to reduce anxiety about unfinished tasks.
- **Healthy Lifestyle Choices**: Avoid excessive caffeine, alcohol, and sugar, which can exacerbate anxiety.

Develop a Routine

Consistency is critical to forming new habits. Incorporate your chosen strategies into your daily routine. For example, start your day with a mindfulness meditation session, use cognitive behavioral techniques when negative thoughts arise, and practice relaxation exercises before bed.

Seek Support

Seek Support: building a support network can provide encouragement and accountability. Share your goals with friends, family, or a support group. Consider working with a therapist who can lead you through the process and help you stay on track. If you're unsure where to start, ask your primary care physician for a referral to a therapist or search online for support groups in your area.

Maintaining Progress and Handling Setbacks

Once you've created a personalized plan and started implementing it, maintaining progress and handling setbacks are crucial for long-term success. Here are some tips to help you stay on course:

Monitor Your Progress

Regularly review your progress to see how far you've come. Keep a journal to track your achievements and any challenges you face. Celebrate your successes, no matter how small, to stay motivated.

Stay Flexible

Life is unpredictable, and rigid plans can lead to frustration. Be open to adjusting your strategies as needed. If a particular technique isn't working for you, try another approach. Flexibility allows you to adapt to modifying circumstances without feeling defeated.

Develop Coping Mechanisms

Setbacks are inevitable, but they don't have to derail your progress. Develop coping mechanisms to deal with challenges. For example, if you are overthinking, use a quick mindfulness exercise to return to the present moment.

Practice Self-Compassion

Overcoming overthinking is a trip, and it's expected to experience ups and downs. Remember, you're not alone in this. Treat yourself with the same compassion you would offer a friend. Acknowledge your efforts and remind yourself that setbacks are part of the process.

Re-evaluate and Adjust Goals

Reevaluate and Adjust Goals: Periodically reassess and adjust your goals as needed. As you progress, you might find that your initial goals no longer fit your current situation. For example, if you initially set a goal to reduce overthinking by 50% in three months but find it too challenging, you can adjust it to a more realistic goal of reducing overthinking by 30%.

Continue Learning and Growing

Stay open to learning new strategies. The more you know, the more equipped you are to manage overthinking. Read books, attend workshops, and seek resources to enhance your understanding of overthinking and provide new management tools. Continuous learning is not just a tool; it's a mindset that keeps you engaged and motivated.

Maintain a Balanced Lifestyle

Maintain a Balanced Lifestyle: a balanced lifestyle supports your mental health. Ensure you sleep well, eat healthy food, exercise regularly, and engage in activities you enjoy. For instance, getting enough sleep can help you think more clearly and reduce stress, while regular exercise can improve your mood and decrease anxiety. Balance work, rest, and play to create a holistic approach to managing overthinking.

Building a sustainable practice to stop overthinking requires a personalized plan, consistent effort, and the flexibility to adapt to challenges. By setting clear goals, choosing appropriate strategies, and maintaining progress through self-compassion and support, you can break free from overthinking and live a more peaceful, present-focused life.

Conclusion

As we conclude our tour through "Stop Overthinking: Proven Strategies to Calm Your Mind, Relieve Stress, and Overcome Anxiety - Break Free and Live in the Moment," you must recognize the significant steps you've taken. Your path, filled with learning and self-discovery, has equipped you with the tools to manage and reduce overthinking. This final chapter is a testament to your growth, reinforcing the key strategies and insights and providing the motivation for the next phase of your journey.

Throughout this book, we've delved into the causes of overthinking, including stress, anxiety, and negative cognitive patterns. Understanding these root causes is essential because it helps you recognize the triggers that prompt overthinking. For instance, if work-related stress or personal relationships are significant triggers for you, acknowledging this is the first step in managing and mitigating their impact.

In terms of daily techniques, we've covered a range of practices to help calm your mind. Mindfulness practices are invaluable tools for grounding yourself in the present moment. These techniques help you break free from the cycle of repetitive negative thoughts by bringing your focus back to the here and now. Cognitive tools like thought records and Socratic questioning are equally important. They enable you to identify and challenge irrational thoughts, replacing them with more realistic perspectives. Additionally, progressive muscle relaxation and guided imagery relieve the tension often accompanying overthinking.

A healthy lifestyle is a cornerstone of mental well-being. Regular exercise improves physical health, significantly boosts mood, and reduces anxiety. A balanced diet rich in nutrients keeps brain function and overall health, while good sleep hygiene ensures your mind and body get the rest they need to function optimally. Time management is another crucial aspect. By prioritizing tasks and keeping your environment organized, you reduce the cognitive pressure on your brain, making it easier to stay calm.

It's critical to acknowledge and celebrate your progress. Overcoming overthinking is not a one-time achievement but an ongoing process. Stay curious and open to new techniques and strategies that can help you manage overthinking. Setting small, achievable goals keeps you motivated and allows you to celebrate progress, no matter how minor it may seem. For instance, if you've successfully practiced mindfulness for ten minutes daily for a week, take a moment to recognize and celebrate this significant step forward in your trip.

Self-compassion is a vital and nurturing part. Be gentle with yourself, especially when you encounter setbacks. Understand that setbacks are a natural part of progress and use them as learning opportunities. Reflect on your progress and be willing to adapt your strategies as needed. Remember, your ability to be flexible and adaptable is a key strength that will help you maintain long-term change.

Your way of managing to overthink is unique and personal. The tools and insights from this book are here to support and guide you, but your commitment and effort will make a difference. Even when it feels challenging, stay persistent. Change takes time and consistent effort, so be patient with yourself. And remember, you're not alone in this. Reach out for support when you need it. Friends, family, and professionals can provide valuable encouragement and perspective, helping you stay on track.

Embrace your trip with an open heart and mind. Recognize and celebrate your progress along the way. Each step you take towards managing overthinking is a victory, no matter how small. Pay attention to living in the present moment and finding joy in everyday experiences. This mindfulness will help you reduce overthinking and enhance your overall quality of life.

In conclusion, stay persistent in your efforts, be kind to yourself, and enjoy the way ahead. Your path is filled with opportunities for growth, happiness, and fulfillment. By applying the strategies and insights from this book, you are well-equipped to embrace a life free from the constraints of overthinking.

Resources

Here are some valuable resources to help you manage and overcome overthinking. These include recommended readings, apps and tools for mindfulness and stress relief, and support groups and professional organizations that can provide additional guidance and support.

Recommended Readings

1. **"The Power of Now" by Eckhart Tolle**

This book emphasizes the importance of living in the present moment and provides practical advice for overcoming overthinking and finding peace.

2. **"Mindfulness in Plain English" by Bhante Henepola Gunaratana**

A straightforward guide to mindfulness meditation, offering techniques that can help reduce stress and anxiety.

3. **"The Happiness Trap" by Dr. Russ Harris**

Based on Acceptance and Commitment Therapy (ACT), this book teaches how to reduce stress and worry through mindfulness and behavioral strategies.

4. **"The Miracle of Mindfulness" by Thich Nhat Hanh**

A classic introduction to mindfulness practice, with practical exercises to help integrate mindfulness into daily life.

5. "Feeling Good: The New Mood Therapy" by Dr. David D. Burns

This book provides cognitive-behavioral techniques to combat negative thinking patterns and improve mental health.

6. "Radical Acceptance" by Tara Brach

Explores how embracing your true self and accepting your emotions can lead to profound emotional healing and reduce overthinking.

Apps and Tools for Mindfulness and Stress Relief

1. **App 'Headspace'**

Offers guided meditation sessions and mindfulness exercises to help reduce stress and improve focus.

2. **App 'Calm'**

Provides a variety of meditations, sleep stories, and breathing exercises to help manage stress and anxiety.

3. **App 'Insight Timer'**

Features a vast library of free guided meditations and mindfulness practices led by experienced teachers.

4. **App 'Ten Percent Happier'**

Focuses on making mindfulness meditation accessible and practical with guided sessions and courses.

5. **App 'Smiling Mind'**

Provides mindfulness and meditation programs designed for different age groups and settings, including work and school.

Support Groups and Professional Organizations

1. **Anxiety and Depression Association of America (ADAA)**

Provides resources, support groups, and information on finding professional help for anxiety and related disorders.

2. **National Alliance on Mental Illness (NAMI)**

Offers support groups, educational resources, and advocacy for individuals with mental health conditions and their families.

3. **Mindful Schools**

Provides mindfulness training and resources for educators, students, and parents to help integrate mindfulness into school communities.

4. **Mental Health America (MHA)**

Offers a variety of mental health resources, including screening tools, support groups, and information on finding local help.

5. **The Mindfulness Center**

Provides training, retreats, and resources for individuals looking to deepen their mindfulness practice.

6. **Association for Behavioral and Cognitive Therapies (ABCT)**

Offers resources to find trained cognitive-behavioral therapists and information on CBT practices.